Bubbletecture

Bubbletecture

....

Inflatable Architecture and Design

Sharon Francis

Introduction
07

Bubbletecture
14

Index
272

Introduction

Innovative, revolutionary and often avant-garde, inflatable objects and structures are imbued with political, cultural or social significance. By their very nature, they are an expression of advancement; a reimagining of traditional forms. Influential in aviation for more than two centuries, this deceptively simple technology has in recent decades been at the forefront of architectural movements, enabled cutting-edge artistic practice and has been symbolic of technological utopianism.

Bubbletecture is a select compendium of inflatables now. Showcasing more than two hundred works, this book features projects that span the realms of architecture, art, design and fashion from the 1960s through to the present day. In this introduction the back-catalogue of pneumatics is delved into — a potted history of sorts — illuminating the appeal, potential and wide application of inflatable technology, giving context to the surprising array of materials, forms, colours, sizes and locations of pneumatics today. While bouncy castles and pool floats might be the populist face of blow-up objects, this book vividly demonstrates that the world of inflatables is far richer.

The First Inflatables

The invention of the first inflatable — the hot-air balloon — came about in the mid-eighteenth century in France. At this time, Paris was the cultural junction of the intellectual and philosophical movement known as The Enlightenment,

which took place from 1715 to 1789, the latter being the year of the French Revolution. Philosophical and scientific enquiry abounded, led by prolific writer and poet Voltaire and later influenced by the ruminations of René Descartes. These philosophers argued for a society based upon natural law and scientific reasoning. The Enlightenment succeeded in bringing about a paradigm shift in French culture, felt across Europe, which moved thought towards science and reductionism, and away from religious dogma.

It was in this climate in 1782 that the French brothers Joseph-Michel and Jacques-Étienne Montgolfier created the first hot-air balloon by burning straw and wool to heat air under a large, lightweight paper and fabric bag. A year later, the first manned, untethered flight took place with passengers Jean-François Pilâtre de Rozier and Marquis François Laurent d'Arlandes flying over Paris for about fifteen minutes.

In 1784 Jean Baptiste Meusnier, recognized as the father of modern dirigibles, or airships, was the first to propose the familiar cigar-shaped crafts still used today. It was not until Count Ferdinand von Zeppelin, a German nobleman and army general, devoted himself to their development that airships became successful. Working with a team of engineers, he created the Luftschiff Zeppelin 1 — commonly referred to as LZ1 — in 1893. At 128 m (420 ft) long, it was the largest object ever built to fly. The internal aluminium frame allowed the airships to be larger, more weather-resistant and travel faster.

The LZ1 was launched in front of a crowd of 12,000 in 1900 and, despite some technical hitches, this flight heralded the so-called 'golden age' of air transport.

Zeppelins continued to be developed and manufactured and were used extensively by the Germans during World War I in bombing raids over cities, including in London and Paris. The Zeppelins went from strength to strength in the post-war period until the infamous Hindenburg disaster of 1937. The largest airship ever built, the Hindenburg's tail burst into flames while landing in the US after a transatlantic flight — a disaster that all but brought about the demise of the dirigible industry.

Twentieth-Century Ballooning

In 1932 Auguste Piccard, a Swiss scientist, undertook the first manned flight into near-space in a helium balloon, reaching a record-breaking 16 km (9.94 mi) high. Over the next few years records continued to be set and broken. In 1935 Explorer II, a helium balloon with a sealed cabin, manned by US Army Captains Albert Stevens and Orvil Anderson, reached an altitude of 22 km (13.6 mi). This highly publicized flight became a milestone in aviation history, establishing that human survival within a pressurized chamber was possible, and paving the way for future space travel.

In 1978 and 1981, respectively, the first Atlantic and Pacific crossings in a helium balloon were made, setting new duration and distance records each time. Balloon flight came full circle, with a return to hot-air ballooning when UK

businessman and adventurer Richard Branson and Swedish aeronautical engineer Per Lindstrand crossed the Atlantic in 1987 in the largest balloon ever flown. The duo followed this with a Pacific crossing in 1991, reaching record-breaking speeds of up to 395 km (245 mi) per hour.

In February 1995 American aviator and adventurer Steve Fossett made the first solo transatlantic flight, travelling from Korea to Canada. Eventually succeeding on his sixth attempt, in 2002, he was the first person to fly an uninterrupted, unrefuelled, solo circumnavigation of the globe in any form of aircraft.

Warfare

From 1794 to 1945 balloons were predominantly used in warfare. In the US Civil War and through World Wars I and II, balloons were tools for surveillance, transportation, communication and weaponry.

During 1944 and 1945 1,100 men of the 23rd Headquarters Special Troops, known as the Ghost Army, an elite unit whose speciality was tactical deception, staged more than twenty battlefield deceptions using inflatable tanks. Their role was to create the impression that the allied forces were bigger and more powerful than they actually were. Inflatable tanks, together with rubber airplanes and elaborate costumes, were deployed in combination with a soundtrack of armoured and infantry units broadcast via powerful amplifiers. It is now estimated that the Ghost Army saved tens of thousands of lives and was instrumental in a number of Allied victories in Europe.

Inflatable Structures

Initially created for the US military, the first basic inflatable structure was designed by engineer Walter Bird in the Cornell Aeronautical Lab. His radomes — a structural, weatherproof enclosure — were used to protect radar antennae. Hundreds were utilized during the late 1940s and 1950s. Bird set up Birdair Structures Inc. in Buffalo, New York in 1956, developing inflatables that included storage sheds, greenhouses and pool enclosures. These products raised the profile and potential of inflatables, and caught the attention of architects, leading Bird on to numerous collaborations.

In the late 1950s — the same period as the design and construction of the Guggenheim in New York City — Frank Lloyd Wright took an experimental deviation to explore a prototype for an inflatable village. In an attempt to create a model of affordable housing — a concern he revisited from time to time — the Fiberthin Air Houses were conceived. The hemispheres were constructed from vinyl-coated nylon fabric and supported by low-pressure air that was provided by a fan-driven heating and cooling system.

The 1960s

Not since the post-war Modernist social utopias imagined in Europe in the 1920s had there been such a spirit of change to emerge as in the 1960s. It was in this anti-establishment environment that a second wave of utopian architecture took off across Europe and the US. Cheap, mass-produced plastic had become widely available, making exploration of the potential of inflatables an appealing possibility. Young, radical architecture groups embraced the creative potential of inflatable technology, whether as a vehicle for dissent against the conventions of traditional architectural education, or in reaction to the pervading Brutalist movement of the time.

This experimental vision was fuelled by the counter-culture movement and happened within the context of the first space explorations. Architects and artists at the forefront of this movement include collaboratives such as Austrian firms Coop Himmelb(l)au and Haus-Rucker-Co (page 181), Ant Farm in the US (page 223) and Archigram in the UK (page 194).

With their dwelling prototype Villa Rosa, 1968, Coop Himmelb(l)au used the potential of pneumatic structures to explore habitation and modes of existence within the city. Restless Sphere, 1971, was an interactive transparent orb, 4 m (13 ft) in diameter, which served as a performance piece within the city streets of Basel, Switzerland — set into action by a person walking inside. Around the same time, Spatial Effects were experimenting with their Waterwalk series (page 162) that performed similarly on water.

Haus-Rucker-Co's parasitic bubble Oase No. 7, which was installed, sucker-like, on the side the Museum of Art and Trade in Kassel, Germany in 1972, explored the creation of utopian environments through experimental installations that altered perceptions and expectations of space. At the same time, their inflatable model for living, Gelbes Herz (Yellow Heart), designed in 1967 — a pneumatic space capsule featuring a small chamber with a transparent plastic mattress that sleeps two people — was intended as a critique of the static nature and monumentality of contemporary architecture.

In 1972 the reactionary architecture group Ant Farm drew attention to issues of environmental sustainability when they created the Clean Air Pod (page 223). Ahead of their time in consideration of ecological issues, Ant Farm proposed an architecture that was inexpensive, transportable and almost instantaneous, challenging the constructs of traditional form and identity.

Archigram's wildly imaginative Cushicle and Suitaloon projects, designed in 1964 and 1967 respectively, proposed a new relationship between the individual and the city — the suits, when inflated, enabled people to carry a complete environment on their body.

Art

Some inflatable artworks serve as architectural interventions, transforming and reinterpreting the spaces they inhabit. The work of collective Penique Productions — such as El Claustro (page 196) — often articulates the architectural details of the spaces they inhabit, while the site-specific work of Alex Schweder, including Wall To Wall, Floor to Ceiling (page 264), extrapolates and reconfigures the built environment

for which it was developed. The RedBall Project by Kurt Perschke (page 100) is a series of interventions in which a giant sphere is wedged and squeezed into various architectural contexts, altering perceptions of the built environment through humour and surprise.

Other inflatable artworks have sought to extend the boundaries of the achievable, while at the same time generating awe and delight. Environmental artist Christo's monumental Big Air Package (page 134), a thing of wonder and fragility, was also, temporarily, the largest self-supporting structure in the world.

Plastique Fantastique's Sound of Light (page 132) utilized technology to capture light waves, translating them to sound waves to create a unique experiential colour-infused soundscape, while Osmo by Loop.pH (page 202) provided a transportable projected universe of nearly 3,000 stars for city dwellers. TeamLab's Homogenizing and Transforming World (page 94) immersed visitors within a mass of giant, colour-shifting floating spheres that communicated with each other wirelessly.

Furniture

Since the mass availability of plastic in the 1960s, the inflatable chair has been an object of periodic exploration and invention. The Zanotta Blow Chair (page 130) and Quasar Khanh's seating range (page 172) were among the first lightweight, inexpensive, commercially available products to be mass produced, becoming design icons of their time. Marcel Wanders' Balloon Chair (page 65),

Tehila Guy's Anda blow-up chair (page 98) and the Womanly seat by Kiri-Una Brito Meumann (page 22) demonstrate designers responding to new paradigms in fashion and materiality, all with a degree of whimsy. Zieta Prozessdesign's range of Plopp stools (page 224) follows in the tradition, but utilizes a unique process in which air is forced into an opening between two fine sheets of steel to create a quirky, stable, inflated product.

Fashion

While fashion has seen some kooky inflated garments, the hybrid pieces that straddle fashion, art and function provide an interesting genre. In the tradition of Archigram's Suitaloon, Ana Rewakowicz's Sleeping Bag Dress (page 194) transforms from a kimono-style dress into a sleeping bag, allowing the wearer to carry their 'home' on their back. The Transformable C.P. Company Armchair Jacket by designer Moreno Ferrari (page 192) inflates from a longline jacket into a convenient armchair. Anna Maria Cornelia's Life Dress (page 213) while whimsical, and hardly practical, provides a commentary on the often suffocating nature of contemporary urban life.

Architecture

While single-membrane inflated structures remain in the domain of the temporary, various technologies have been developed to create double-walled membranes that have become part of more permanent building systems for composite pneumatic structures.

Among these are ETFE (ethylene tetrafluoroethylene) panels. A fluorine-based plastic, it is durable, recyclable, highly transparent, corrosion-resistant and very lightweight in comparison to glass structures. Its true potential was evident after its application in the Eden Project (page 106) by Grimshaw Architects in 1998. The Allianz Arena by Herzog & De Meuron (page 146) constructed for the 2006 FIFA World Cup, and the Water Cube, built for the 2008 Beijing Summer Olympics (page 26), raised the profile of the technology, and proved it to be an innovative, sustainable building material.

At the time of going to press, Diller Scofidio + Renfro's adventurous new-build, The Shed, was under construction in New York City. The building, designed as an arts centre, features a telescoping outer shell, made from ETFE systems, which can be deployed from its position over the base building, gliding along rails onto an adjoining plaza to double the footprint of the building.

Social Responsibility

The immediacy and inexpensive nature of inflatable products means that they can provide solutions in emergency situations, or where socio-cultural need exists. Michael Rakowitz's *paraSITE* shelters (page 222) provided cheap, heated housing for the homeless. Alice Chun's SolarPuff inflatable light (page 251) and the Luci solar-powered lantern by MPOWERD (page 161) both respond to the need for basic lighting sources in developing countries. Illumination transforms lives in simple but dramatic ways by, for example, allowing children to continue to read at night.

On a different scale, Ark Nova (page 88), a collaboration between architect Arata Isozaki and artist Anish Kapoor, provided a mobile performance and exhibition space to unite communities still rebuilding after the devastation caused when a major earthquake and tsunami hit Japan in 2011.

The Future

New materials and systems are always under development, creating myriad possibilities for inflatables in the future.

The Diodon Project (page 215), for example, created by French student collective Dynamorphe, prototyped a new construction system combining an inflatable with an auxetic material that has the capacity to shrink, expand and multiply via real-time digital control. The inflatables of Chico MacMurtrie, recognized for his large-scale kinetic installations such as *Chrysalis* (page 248), integrate amorphic robotic systems that are interactive on multiple levels, simulating the architecture of the human body.

New 'Balloons'

Among a number of near-space and stratospheric projects underway is Google's Loon (page 169), a network of polyethylene balloons carrying remote-controlled solar-powered electronics systems that beam down high-speed Internet coverage to remote areas.

Since 2011 the American aerospace and defence company Lockheed Martin

has continued to develop and test its High Altitude Airship (HAA) — unmanned, helium-filled vehicles that operate above the jet-stream in a geostationary position for telecommunications, surveillance and weather monitoring.

Elsewhere, Barcelona-based Zero2infinity are simplifying space access with the Bloostar, a prototype rocket that launches from a balloon which has ascended to 25 km (15.5 mi). Satellites at these altitudes facilitate transmission and collection of information as well as scientific research and testing. The possibilities for stratospheric balloons include power generation, communications, data collection, security, weather forecasting and Earth observations. Zero2infinity's Bloon stratospheric balloon is also in development, working towards offering commercial trips for six people — two pilots and four passengers — up to an altitude of 36 km (22 mi) from bases in Spain.

Technologies in Development

In 2017 MIT Media Lab's Tangible Group developed a system, called AeroMorph, which, with minimal human interaction, folds paper, plastic and fabric into various origami shapes when inflated. The methodology has a range of potential applications in wearables, toys, automated packaging and even building systems.

Intelligent pneumatic systems have the potential to respond to environmental conditions in real-time. A research team at the Institute for Advanced Architecture in Catalonia, Spain, has developed a construction 'skin' that does just this, to allow active adjustment to fluctuations in the environment. Various materials, including silicon and fabric, have been tested for suitability, allowing dozens of cells to inflate or deflate, reducing wind vibrations and drag and controlling light infiltration.

The Next Frontier

In a competition backed by NASA, architectural firm Foster and Partners created a conceptual, modular habitat for Mars. The proposed dwelling is constructed robotically prior to the arrival of the astronauts; semi-autonomous robots then select the site and dig a crater, allowing inflatable modules to sit within it, forming the core of the dwelling. The inflatables are rapidly deployed and provide stability despite uneven ground conditions. 3D-printed components, made from the excavated soil and rocks, complete the construction.

NASA scientists working in collaboration with researchers from the agriculture department of the University of Arizona in Tucson, USA have developed an inflatable Lunar/Martian greenhouse prototype that allows vegetables to be grown in deep space. Carbon dioxide exhaled by astronauts is used by the plants for photosynthesis in what is called a 'bioregenerative life support system'. The system is also designed to be used for air revitalization, and water and waste recycling.

The possibilities for future development and use, in and beyond the digital age, have the potential to expand as new frontiers, materials and processes seek to exploit the versatile, lightweight and sustainable nature of inflatable products. Having established itself within the domain of exploration and experimentation — from the very first steps of aviation to cutting-edge fashion — the blow up serves to blow out traditional forms and perceptions. 'Bubbletecture' is thought-provoking and constantly evolving; this book is a visual ode to its tremendous variety and a celebration of the curiosity it inspires.

Notes

Bubbletecture includes a number of special features, as follows: at the top of each project is the name of the design, followed by the name of the architect, artist or designer who created it. Next to this is a balloon icon that identifies the scale of the project, from small to large. At the back of the book is a Directory of Architects, Artists and Designers.

'This world's a bubble.'
Francis Bacon

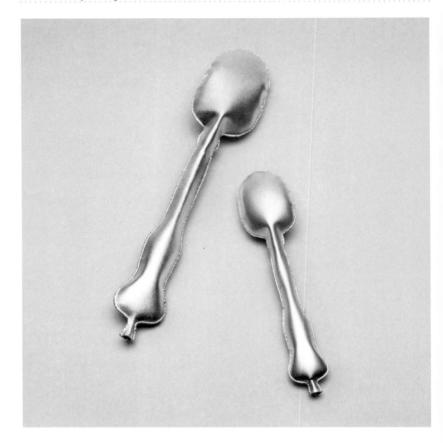

Designer Kim Buck produces inflatable jewellery and tableware alongside his more traditional collections. His silver Hollowware bowl is crafted from metalized plastic foil, while products such as the Puffed Up Vase and Dobbeltriflet Opblæst spoons are crafted from thin silver sheet that has been welded and filled with air. Buck says of his inflatable designs: 'Many see jewellery and hollowware as investments in materials — gold, silver and precious stones. As an artist, I have used irony to distance myself from these mechanisms, insisting that the value of my works lies in their idea, design and execution.'

The nebulous, globular ReFractor is Seattle Design Nerds' answer to engaging the public and invigorating under-used urban areas. Delivered by cart and erected by hand, the installation is made from scavenged plastic and space blankets. Cut into standard triangles, the units join to form a contained building block. With a resilient base of layered cardboard, the varied skin of the inflatable form acts in distinct ways — its hazy plastic diffuses interior light while Mylar segments reflect the surroundings. Its conspicuous form attracts attention, becoming a captivating space for a range of public events.

Project name: **Rendez-vous avec la Vi(II)e**
Architect: **Hans-Walter Müller**
Location: **Paris, France** Date: **2014**

Lightweight, movable and full of air, this temporary structure created an eye-catching feature overlooking Martin Luther King Park in Batignolles, Paris. Designed to house a three-day exhibition, *The Making of Batignolles*, the inflatable pavilion created a bright waterproof area enclosing maquettes, videos and prototypes that explained the future of the redevelopment of the area. Spanning 16 m (53 ft), the dome was set up between two stabilizing entry points. Secured around the perimeter, the project swiftly reached its full height with the aid of an air pump, creating a pavilion with panoramic 360-degree views.

Using a room in her apartment in Montréal, Canada, as a mould, artist Ana Rewakowicz covered all surfaces with multiple coats of rubber liquid latex until a significant thickness built up. After peeling away the imprint, Rewakowicz was left with a transportable skin, complete with architectural details and other remains, such as dirt and hair. This 'skin' was then connected to an external second layer for support, allowing the room to be inflated. Recreated in galleries as a 'room within a room', *Inside Out* is an installation that, when separated from origination, is both disconcerting and playful.

For this interactive installation, artist Alex Schweder inserted an over-inflated archway into the existing structural portal of a gallery space. The arch provided a tight, yet accessible, passage until it deflated and was replaced by the inverted, mirror-version archway above. The two identical archways passed air back and forth between each other continuously, one deflating as the other expanded with the shared air. Examining the constraints of architectural space, the passageway became a volatile place of engagement, alternately accessible then non-existent. It is now part of San Francisco Museum of Modern Art's (SFMOMA) permanent collection.

Melbourne-based artist Kiri-Una Brito Meumann traditionally creates large-scale sculptures that examine the impact of technology and 'life on the Internet'. Her first piece of furniture, this smart, off-beat chair, called Womanly, is constructed from a powder-coated steel framework and features solid oak legs. Cut-outs in the dark-green body allow a series of latex balloons to bulge out in various organic forms. The work contrasts notions of hard and soft, as well as masculine and feminine energy — the melding of steel and latex is one representation of these attributes. The balloons are intended to deflate over time.

Part of artist Charles Petillon's 'Invasions' series, it took 100,000 white balloons to create the joyful *Heartbeat* installation in London's Covent Garden Market Building. Extending 54 m (177 ft), the balloons were fixed onto a steel frame, producing a giant ephemeral cloud that floated above the walkways and sunken arcades of the nineteenth-century building. A warm white light illuminated the structure and gently pulsed like a heartbeat, hence the name. The aim of the piece, according to Petillon, was to 'change the way in which we see the things we live alongside each day without really noticing them'.

Pointed was created as part of a trio of works (page 262), called *XXX*, intended to disrupt and transform visitors' perceptions of its eighteenth-century setting at Mellerstain House in Gordan, Scotland, UK. The environmental artist Steve Messam sought to establish a playful dialogue between the old and the new with this surprising and delightful intervention. Evoking the outline of a stylized explosion or starburst, the white inflatable cones emerged from the pitched roofline of a centuries-old stone building. The twenty-eight elongated peaks rose more than 3 m (10 ft) into the air, providing a bold, sculptural presence within the picturesque park.

Project name: **Peace**
Architect: **Slow Studio**
Location: **Tokyo, Japan** Date: **2016**

This inflatable, spherical sculpture by Japanese architecture practice Slow Studio presented a hostile exterior, supported as it was by large conical spikes. However this presence was overcome as soon as the visitor went beyond the forbidding outer shell, entering through a narrow vertical slot into the orb's cool, white interior. The double-layer membrane created a cushioned, womb-like retreat; a place intended for comfort and contemplation. Standing about 3 m (10 ft) high, the pavilion has been inflated in locations around China and Japan, from expansive greenfield sites to urban spaces. Here, it is pictured in a courtyard in Daikanyama, Tokyo.

Project name: **Water Cube**
Architect: **PTW Architects and others**
Location: **Beijing, China** Date: **2008**

The Beijing National Aquatics Centre, more commonly known as the Water Cube, was created for the 2008 Summer Olympic Games in Beijing, China, with a capacity of 17,000. The building's outer wall design is based on the Weaire-Phelan structure, devised from the natural pattern of bubbles in soap lather. Comprising a steel frame, the Water Cube features a facade of 4,000 ETFE (ethylene tetrafluoroethylene) air-filled bubbles in fifteen different sizes — some more than 9 m (30 ft) across — which made it the world's single largest ETFE-clad structure at the time of construction.

Project name: **Ca.Mia**
Designer: **Denis Santachiara for Campeggi**
Location: **Milan, Italy** Date: **2016**

Designed by Italian maker Denis Santachiara for Campeggi, this brightly coloured emergency bed was created as an antidote to more pragmatic, makeshift options. Combining privacy with ventilation and insect protection, the fun, house-shaped pop up is equipped with an inflatable mattress. The bed can be filled with air by a standard bed pump; packed down, the assemblage is easily transported in a simple carry bag. When erected, the Ca.Mia measures 187 cm (3¼ ft) in length, 103 cm (3½ ft) in width and 100 cm (3¼ ft) in height to the ridgeline of the roof.

Project name: **Media-ICT Building**
Architect: **Cloud 9**
Location: **Barcelona, Spain** Date: **2011**

Commissioned for the 22@Barcelona district, a city zone that promotes ICT (information and communication technology) building models, this project utilizes renewable energy sources, a green roof and solar panels to reduce carbon emissions by ninety-five per cent. The building is equipped with multiple temperature sensors that collect exterior information to adjust interior conditions; ETFE (ethylene tetrafluoroethylene) clad pneumatic panels open in winter to gain solar energy and close in summer to protect and shade. In the south-west facade, nitrogen-based fog is introduced into the panels to give greater opacity.

Project name: **Peace Pavilion**
Architect: **Atelier Zündel Cristea**
Location: **London, England, UK** Date: **2013**

Constructed in a garden adjacent to the Museum of Childhood in London's Bethnal Green, this playful structure won first prize in a summer pavilion competition sponsored by ArchTriumph in 2013. The 62 sq m (203 sq ft) project was self-supporting, bound by an inflatable white tube that rested at three points on an anodized aluminium platform. A clear plastic sheet spanned the snake-like loop and was zipped to the inflated frame, forming an undulating plane that provided shelter and which children could climb across. Its symmetrical form was intended to convey a state of peaceful equilibrium.

This travelling museum was part of a programme that aimed to educate elementary school students about the ancient pre-Columbian societies of Mexico, connecting those peoples and traditions to contemporary life. Rather than house these exhibits in a traditional museum, the inflatable pavilion allowed many more children to access information by taking the museum to them. The translucent structure was extremely lightweight and easily transportable, with a 22 m (72 ft) long digitally printed graphic wall and an open, flexible learning space. The structure itself served as an educational exemplar of the efficiency and sustainability of inflatable architecture.

Shinseon Play comprised more than fifty huge inflatables, each with narrow, steel-pipe stems and bulbous tops. The installation was designed by a collective of architects and installed outside the National Museum of Modern and Contemporary Art in Seoul, South Korea. Based on the ancient Asian myth of Shinseon — hermetic creatures said to live on top of the highest mountains or above the clouds — the work is intended to represent a heavenly landscape that 'transcends the hustle-bustle of the human world of joy, anger, sorrow and pleasure'. A wooden bridge snaked through the canopy, allowing visitors to experience the space from above and below.

In protest of Donald Trump's visit to the UK in 2018, this 6 m (19½ ft) high inflatable doppelgänger baby of the US president was launched in Parliament Square Garden, adjacent to the Houses of Parliament in London, England. The giant balloon, financed via a crowd-funding campaign, was the brainchild of a group of Londoners calling themselves the Trump Babysitters. One of the creators, environmental activist Leo Murray, said: 'Ridiculing tyrants and despots is a proud British tradition ... If this generation is going to have to fight fascism again, we may as well have a bit of a laugh while we are doing it.'

Situated inside the Santiago Calatrava-designed Museum of Arts and Sciences in Valencia, Spain, this multi-inflatable installation filled a huge concourse space with 6 m (20 ft) wide futuristic, opaque pods, which appeared at home beneath the sleek ribbed canopy of the building. Designed by Berlin-based group Plastique Fantastique, a collective known for creating temporary architecture that samples the performative possibilities of urban environments, the pneumatic miniGAGARIN encouraged visitors to the museum to explore new shapes and perspectives through the acid green-tinted portholes.

Project name: **Thirst Pavilion**
Architect: **Cloud 9**
Location: **Zaragoza, Spain** Date: **2008**

In response to the theme of 'Water and Sustainable Development' at the International Expo in Zaragoza, Spain, this 36¼ m (120 ft) diameter, 10 m (33 ft) high igloo was intended to represent the water drops on top of a salt mountain. The pavilion was a commentary on the universal condition of thirst, and showcased exhibits and innovative design solutions for dealing with health-based or drought-related water issues. The primary material was air-filled ETFE (ethylene tetrafluoroethylene) panels that allowed for the creation of the bubble forms. The structure was designed to be disassembled and reassembled for relocation.

This Bubble Dome is one of a series of Pneumatic Masonry inflatables created as a modular system by US-based design collective Pneuhaus. The basic units are air-filled bubbles held together by a network of fabric webbing. The modules can be shaped to create many different forms; this iteration consists of triangles, pentagons and hexagons arranged in a geodesic geometry. Pneuhaus devised a system in which the inflatable structures could be insulated and heated, resulting in durable and semi-permanent constructions that can be used as greenhouses, pavilions, car garages and garden shelters.

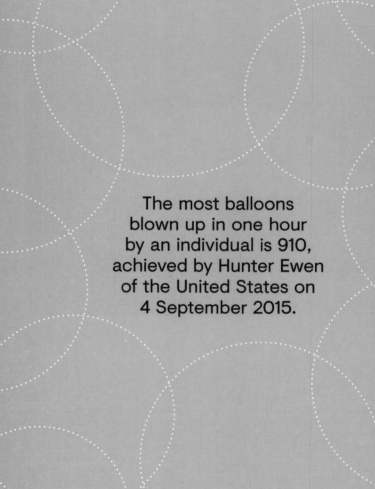

The most balloons
blown up in one hour
by an individual is 910,
achieved by Hunter Ewen
of the United States on
4 September 2015.

Project name: **Inflatable Jacket**
Designer: **Christopher Raeburn**
Location: **London, England, UK** Date: **2015**

London-based fashion designer Christopher Raeburn used material salvaged from an inflatable life raft to create outerwear and accessories reflecting the themes of survival and endurance for his Autumn (Fall) 2015 menswear collection. An all-black rubber field jacket was crafted from the underside of a life raft, while the more colourful panels of the vessel were reworked into a red backpack and a shark-shaped holdall. Continuing with the same theme, latex rubber was used to create inflatable puffer jackets and gilets, blown up using the plastic valves found on swimming armbands.

Project name: **Shelter**
Architect: **Leopold Banchini with Daniel Zamarbide**
Location: **Geneva, Switzerland** Date: **2016**

This transportable nightclub, made from a black PVC membrane, was commissioned by the Federation of Swiss Architects (FSA), also known as the Bund Schweizer Architekten, to host their annual summer party. The blow-up structure contained a bar and dance floor, as well as an assortment of inflatable furniture including seating, tables and a DJ booth. The work explored philosophical and spatial aspects of 'the underground', as examined by theorists including Gaston Bachelard, Paul Virilio and Beatriz Colomina. With its pitch black interior, Shelter was designed to create a deliberately disorientating experience.

Project name: **DesertSeal**
Architect: **Andreas Vogler**
Location: **Germany** Date: **2004**

Devised to survive extreme arid terrain, the DesertSeal is an inflatable, reflective shell in which users can endure soaring temperatures in comfort. Designed according to the thermodynamics of such environments, where air at upper levels is cooler than that close to the sand, the tapered body includes an intake source at the apex and an expelling fan at the base, both powered by a flexible band of solar cells. Lightweight and easily transported, its silver skin reflects piercing heat and contains a narrow space for rest, just over 1 m (3 ft) wide. Though developed on earth, this glistening hybrid might just have the potential to cater to human life on Mars.

Project name: **The Wedge**
Designer: **Heimplanet**
Location: **Germany** Date: **2013**

Allowing campers to spend less time pitching up and more time adventuring, the founders of Heimplanet bring their love of the great outdoors to The Wedge — a two-man tent with inflatable poles. Comprised of three connected air frames that can be erected with a single pump, The Wedge is speedy to inflate and easy to collapse. Weighing just over 3 kg (7 lb) it is a light, practical companion for exploring the outdoors, with a highly waterproof shell that resists rain and dew. Outside, it captures attention for its azure skin; inside, it is filled with light, and includes helpful pockets for holding your kit.

Project name: **Tafla Mirrors**
Designer: **Zieta Prozessdesign Studio**
Location: **Wrocław, Poland** Date: **2015**

This series of mirrors, which appear like oversized pebbles as a result of their flat, organic forms, are crafted using FIDU technology, developed by Polish design studio Zieta, and used to produce a range of seating, as well as large-scale structures. The FIDU process involves pumping compressed air into a double membrane of thin steel sheeting that has been welded together; the steel is thin enough to deform but strong enough to hold its shape. The freeform manipulation of the material under pressure means that each mirror is different from the next, resembling large droplets of metal.

Project name: **Sacrilege**
Artist: **Jeremy Deller**
Location: **Glasgow, Scotland, UK** Date: **2012**

The ancient monument of Stonehenge is one of England's busiest tourist destinations but has been roped off since 1977 and can only be viewed from a distance. Consequently, its massive scale is hard to grasp. Turner Prize winner Jeremy Deller's 43 m (140 ft) wide, life-sized, bouncy castle version of the stone edifice flips the paradigm and allows total public access and interaction. A co-commission between Glasgow International Festival of Visual Art and the Mayor of London, *Sacrilege* is playful and irreverent and, as the title suggests, potentially offensive to some.

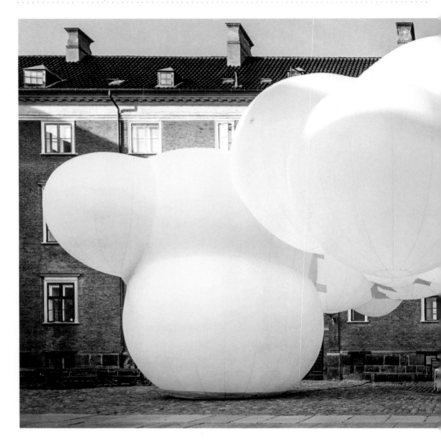

The multiple bubble forms of this structure create an arc that is both shelter and beacon. Called Skum, the Danish word for foam, the inflatable pavilion was designed to be both permanent and transportable and was used for installations at various events across Denmark. Made of the same material as bouncy castles, the architect's intention was to create a whimsical structure reminiscent of the playgrounds of visitors' childhoods. The pavilion can be inflated in just seven minutes, and illuminated by LEDs in a rotating spectrum of colours.

Project name: **Air Lounger**
Designer: **Inflate**
Location: **London, England, UK** Date: **2015**

Compact, self-assembly furniture is now synonymous with wood and plastic products, however iconic design studio Inflate aimed to create the ultimate in flat-pack with this simple seat, called the Air Lounger. The idea was to design an inflated PVC chair that transformed into something that was not necessarily recognisable as a blown up object. The chair's simple, versatile form can be used in its translucent 'naked' state, or a fabric cover can easily be slipped over it, resulting in a rather more finished, upholstered piece of furniture with any number of different looks.

Project name: **Fragile Occupancy Cloud**
Designer: **Hidemi Nishida Studio**
Location: **Los Angeles, California, USA** Date: **2013**

Filling the ceiling of the Mack Sennett Studios in Los Angeles, California, USA, this immersive installation of inflatable 'clouds' transformed the 450 sq m (4,700 sq ft) venue into a dream-like party zone for the launch of the 2013 FYF Fest. Hovering between 2–4 m (6–13 ft) above the floor, the transparent plastic bubbles bobbed and jostled, wave-like, when touched by guests. The density of the 'clouds' was more concentrated over the stage and bar areas, helping to define their locations, with the colour and brightness of the bubbles reacting to the music.

Appearing like a futuristic bouncy castle, designers' Numen/For Use project, Net Blow-Up, featured a sequence of multiple layers of black mesh nets, suspended within a white inflatable form. The inflatable was filled with air until the outer skin had enough tension to stretch the nets tethered within, creating a complex network in which people could move and play. This movement made for an evolving, kinetic formation, which at night was illuminated from within. The inflatable became a projection screen of sorts, casting shadows of the shifting environment inside onto the exterior, in a manner similar to a shadow play.

English fashion designer Gareth Pugh makes an impact with his bold, outlandish and unconventional creations, designing for artists like Lady Gaga, Róisín Murphy and Beyoncé. His Central Saint Martins' graduate show — a bodysuit of inflatable red-and-white striped balloons — was featured on the cover of *Dazed* magazine's April 2004 issue, and was later exhibited alongside work by Stella McCartney and Hussein Chalayan. Inflatable pieces have appeared in many of his collections over the years. This black-and-white striped nylon dress has a small fan built in to the back, which allows the wearer to inflate and deflate the skirt as desired.

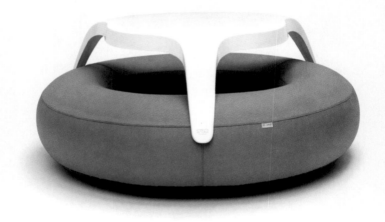

Measuring 190 cm (75 in) in diameter, DoNuts provide table seating for up to six people. The doughnut-shaped tube is made of heavy-duty rubber with a UV-resistant, environmentally friendly polyester coating. This material was developed in the automotive sector, resulting in a highly tested, strong and durable waterproof fabric, which makes the rapidly inflatable seat versatile enough to be at home by the pool but equally suited to a contemporary interior. The removable, polyester-finish table gives this eye-catching piece an appealing edge of practicality.

SuperKOLMEMEN was an urban intervention work by the Berlin-based Plastique Fantastique collective, which popped up in a busy city square as part of Helsinki Design Week. A playful, elliptical inflatable, it was installed around the rather more serious statue of a trio of manual labourers, called *The Three Smiths*, designed by Felix Nylund and erected in 1932. Inside and around the doughnut-like, compressed-air installation, an environment was created where people could gather to talk, dance or relax and participate in a programme of cultural events organized by the festival.

Designer Mario Bellini created these super light armchairs and modular sofas using materials not usually found in the world of padded furniture. The design derives from a packaging technique known as the 'air ravioli' concept, in which the furniture is filled with transparent plastic bubbles of air. The innovative use of materials and processes transforms recycled products into surprisingly elegant and indestructible objects. The covers are made from the stainless-steel mesh of industrial filters, combined with fibre sacks formerly used to transport grain, stones and sugar. The seats feature LEDs embedded within, which cast a colourful glow.

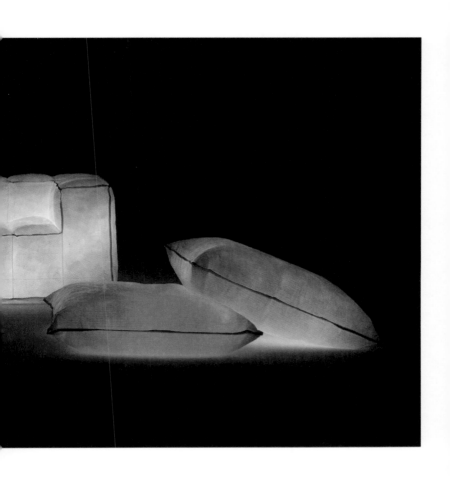

Originally created by two Swedish industrial design students to circumvent the issue of people not wearing bicycle helmets for aesthetic reasons, this inflatable, less invasive, more fashion-friendly solution was tested by researchers at Stanford University. The Hövding airbag is a collar waiting to be a helmet; worn around the users' neck, it resembles a puffy scarf. In the event of a collision, in-built sensors trigger instantaneous inflation and it wraps over the head like a hood to cushion the skull. Made from an ultra-tough nylon fabric, the helmet is also strong enough not to rip when scraped against the ground.

Project name: **Cloud Room Divider**
Designer: **Monica Förster**
Location: **Stockholm, Sweden** Date: **2012**

This light, white, translucent 'room' is intended to mimic the sensation of being among the clouds. Using minimal materials, the simple structure is sustainable, transportable, and can be inflated in about four minutes. Standing at 2 m (7½ ft) high, providing ample space for meetings, focused work, rest or meditation, it has a footprint of approximately 5 x 4 m (17 x 13 ft). What's more, the fluffy cloud can be folded and packed into an average-sized sports bag upon deflation.

Project name: **Blowing Molds**
Designer: **Eden Ohana**
Location: **Tel Aviv, Israel** Date: **2012**

The unusual forms of these lamps are created by a process in which latex is poured into a mould and inflated to make seemingly random shapes, further exhibiting their subtleties when illuminated. Israeli designer Eden Ohana built a specific tool that he calls the 'volume definer' to extend the limits of the material and enable him to control the outcomes. He says: 'The essence and objective of this project was to broaden the limits and limitations of the use of materials and existing objects, as well as the reciprocity and connections between subject and material.'

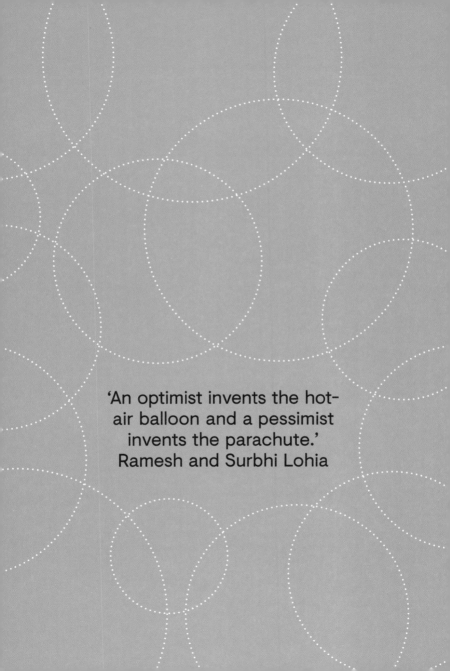

'An optimist invents the hot-air balloon and a pessimist invents the parachute.'
Ramesh and Surbhi Lohia

The architect Luis Pons' floating installation for Art Basel in Miami Beach in 2005 was a commentary on the rise of the so-called McMansion and the parallel culture of consumption that he felt pervaded American society. Seven years later, the villa was re-introduced, this time reflecting the diminished real-estate market. As well as being symbolic of plummeting house values — a consequence of the global financial crisis of 2008 — the deflation was also an analogy for the personal aspect of the experience, mirroring the feelings of powerlessness and fragility that were a result of the crash.

Project name: **A Sac of Rooms All Day Long**
Artist: **Alex Schweder**
Location: **San Francisco, California, USA** Date: **2009**

This installation consisted of the skin of a small 'house', made of clear vinyl, stuffed with four rooms of a second larger 'house', inflating and deflating inside it. The rooms expanded and contracted at different speeds, morphing between something recognizable and then indistinct. The details — such as windows, cornices and stairs — were articulated by black vinyl strips, in the manner of an architectural drawing. An integral sound installation by Los Angeles-based Yann Novak accompanied the expansion and contraction, described by artist Alex Schweder as 'something too big inside something too small'. It is now part of San Francisco Museum of Modern Art's (SFMOMA) permanent collection.

Yohji Yamamoto's Spring 1999 Ready-to-Wear show was a wedding-themed collection and featured a striking, vampish black inflatable skirt, which was removed mid-runway by the model to reveal a sleek tube dress beneath. For designers, inflatable clothing serves to exaggerate form and bring more focus to context and function. 'Behind the wedding dress there must be many stories,' Yamamoto said of the work. A subsequent collection in 2011 also featured inflatable garments, including a whimsical, bright yellow skirt, constructed in the same manner as a plastic pool raft.

This ultra-lightweight chair, created by Dutch designer Marcel Wanders, was conceived with the intention of being the world's lightest seat. Handmade from party balloons filled with compressed air, the form is then wrapped in strips of carbon fibre and hardened with epoxy resin. The fine gridded netting for the seat is also made from carbon fibre. The chair weighs in at a mere 800 g (1.75 lb), is extremely durable and is also sustainable, requiring few materials for its construction and generating minimal waste. Reminiscent of Wanders' Knotted Chair from 1996, it has an elegant form, notable for its simplicity and wit.

Project name: **Luminaria**
Designer: **Architects of Air**
Location: **Various** Date: **1992—present**

Originally developed as a project for people with special needs, Architects of Air founder
Alan Parkinson started experimenting with pneumatic structures in the 1980s. Since the first
Luminarium in 1992, twenty-seven *Luminaria* have toured over forty countries. Inspired by natural
forms, geometric solids, and Islamic and Gothic architecture, each structure is distinctly detailed.
At around 1,000 sq m (10,000 sq ft) in area, they are modular and adaptable to different sites.
Daylight shining through the semi-translucent fabric produces colour-infused, immersive spaces
consisting of maze-like portals, designed to elicit wonder and delight.

This vibrant, lightweight geodesic dome was built from off-the-shelf inflatable beach rings —
symbols of summertime fun. The multi-coloured pavilion was constructed as part of the C!here
Art Crawl in Beijing, forming an intimate space within a public area; in this instance, it sat
within a large housing development in the city. Artist Virginia Melnyk hoped that being inside
the colourful pavilion would provide visitors with a new perspective of their urban surroundings.
After the event, the inflatable pool toys were donated to a charity for local children to enjoy.

Commissioned by the Pawtuckets Arts Festival, Rhode Island, USA, this installation playfully used the concept of the camera obscura. Mimicking the structure of an insect's eye, the 6 m (20 ft) wide inflatable dome consisted of 109 hexagonal bubbles, each containing a pinhole camera. With light filtering through a tiny hole in the centre of each, the result was 109 shifted, inverted images of the surrounding environment being projected onto the translucent lining inside each pocket. Viewers entered the pavilion, with its almost reptilian-like plastic skin, and pushed and squeezed on the bubbles in order to manipulate the images.

These twenty-four inflatable pink objects accompanied by fifteen foam cubes were created for Wolfsburg's State Garden Show by German landscape architects, Topotek 1. The oversized, soft forms were strewn about the lawn like taut skins, their pink hues and indeterminate use attracting the attention of young and old who lolled on, climbed through, rolled with or simply gazed at the unusual bulging objects. In contrast to the natural surroundings of the Allerpark, the pink playground offered a collection of over-scaled toys that are also flexible sculptures — their candyfloss hues can be scattered across any public space, transforming it into a place to play.

Project name: **Dactiloscopia Rosa**
Architect: **Plastique Fantastique**
Location: **Madrid, Spain** Date: **2017**

This playful inflatable, a gigantic, stylized pink hand, was inspired by a blown-up rubber glove. Created as a site-specific installation within the Nave 11 gallery space inside the Matadero Madrid, the 'hand' housed an exhibition of the history of queer fanzines in Spain. Visitors entered at the wrist and were immersed in a luminescent pink glow. Lured towards the flickering of screens at the end of the finger 'tunnels', they then sat in armchairs and viewed various video works. The fingers also provided a representation of the uniqueness of the individual — as evidenced by our fingerprints.

Project name: **Inflatable Dress**
Designer: **Chromat with Klymit**
Location: **New York City, New York, USA** Date: **2017**

Chromat founder Becca McCharen-Tran draws from her background in architecture to produce garments that utilize innovative production techniques and cutting-edge fabrics. As part of Chromat's Fall 2017 collection, McCharen-Tran collaborated with Utah-based outdoor brand Klymit, best known for their ultra-lightweight, cage-like camping pods. This bold red strapless dress — shown alongside a bubbly grey tube top and a lime green vest with cut-out panels — was part of an inflatable collection that used survivalist symbolism (rafts and life jackets) to represent the idea of staying afloat in a tumultuous political environment.

Project name: **Caterpillar Tent**
Artist/Designer: **Lambert Kamps**
Location: **Groningen, The Netherlands** Date: **2007**

The Caterpillar is an itinerant, inflatable film theatre. Set up in parks and festivals to provide sheltered cover, the roving project commands attention with its pillowy red form. Built from PVC foil and shaped by steel cable connections, the double-walled skin becomes taut and supportive as it fills with air. Creating a comfortable environment for movies in hot or wet weather, the tunnel is strong enough to withstand wind and water. Its curious caterpillar 'feet' are stable as well as lightweight and unobtrusive. With a large screen at one end and room for up to thirty people, the nomadic caterpillar creates a memorable night out at the movies.

This curvaceous inflatable structure was installed within a gigantic decommissioned hangar at Tempelhof Airport in Berlin, Germany. Designed as a unique environment within an unusual context, its purpose was to host corporate workshops for the technology company Philips. The 32 m (104 ft) long and 11 m (36 ft) high cloud provided 300 sq m (3,230 sq ft) of space. Divided into three sections, it featured all-white interiors that appeared surreal and almost boundless, juxtaposed with the industrial setting.

Exhibited in the Nordic Pavilion at the Venice Biennale of Architecture 2018, these four inflatables explored the relationship between nature and the built environment, their bulbous forms connected to the building by a tangle of umbilical-like cables. Resembling biological cells, the shapes contained smaller translucent forms. Activated by sensors that monitored carbon dioxide levels, humidity and temperature, the cells took on a life of their own, responding to environmental conditions; when the carbon dioxide levels altered, they expanded or contracted, as if breathing. Temperature fluctuations were evidenced by a changeable glow of colour within.

Project name: **Villa Walala Exchange Square**
Artist: **Camille Walala**
Location: **London, England, UK** Date: **2017**

Created as a site-specific installation for the London Design Festival, this brightly coloured, inflatable castle provided a place for city workers to disconnect and de-stress. Located within a busy park, the installation was made of 1,200 sq m (13,000 sq ft) of vinyl material, patterned with a mix of stripes, circles and blocks in a total of seven different colours. Reminiscent of childhood playgrounds and over-scaled toys, Camille Walala's forms and totems aimed to encourage people to step away from everyday life into a moment altogether more whimsical and calming.

Since the advent of commercially accessible plastics in the 1960s and the arrival of products
such as the iconic Zanotta Blow Chair (page 130), there has been fluctuating public interest in
inflatable furniture. Regardless, designs have continued to evolve both aesthetically and practically,
and one product that has continued to go from strength to strength is the pool float. Air Flower
riffs on the style of chairs popular in the 1960s but has an even more pronounced element of
whimsy. Composed of seven tubular bubbles that create a simple yet functional, flower-like form,
it functions as an outdoor chair and pool float, all rolled into one.

Project name: **playLAND**
Architect: **LIKEArchitects**
Location: **Paredes de Coura, Portugal** Date: **2014**

LIKEArchitects' multi-coloured, spatial interventions for O Mundo ao Contrário (which means The World Turned Upside Down) — a week-long event that transformed a village in northern Portugal into a playground for children — took three different forms. The first was a stage for performances; the second, a silo-shaped tower, which could be entered and explored; and the third a small tunnel (above), for children to run through. The structures, collectively called playLAND, were made of green, orange and pink inflatable beach rings tied together. Removed from their usual context, the rings transformed into vibrant, modular construction elements.

This multi-coloured installation with an elephantine form was commissioned by the Art Production Fund and The Standard Hotel, New York, USA and spanned the full length of the hotel's plaza for a month. Standing 7½ m (25 ft) high and measuring 17 m (55 ft) long, the Light Cave was imagined as a fully immersive experience for guests to pass through into the hotel and for visitors on the High Line, the city's elevated linear park, to wonder at. At night, the amorphous body was lit from within creating a pulsating, glowing spectacle.

Measuring 32 m (105 ft),
the world's longest bubble was
created by Alan McKay of Wellington,
New Zealand on 9 August 1996.
He made it using a bubble wand,
washing-up liquid, glycerine
and water.

Located in the scenic harbour of Antwerp, Belgium, this inflatable structure shelters a rooftop bar on the Badboot boat, which also features one of the largest floating swimming pools in the world. The custom-made, prefabricated inflatable cabin is completely insulated and heated throughout the winter, with transparent cladding that allows the sunlight to permeate and providing a view of the surroundings in a weathertight environment. During the evening, the bar is illuminated from within. Measuring 9 m (30 ft) wide by 18 m (60 ft) long, the clear, air-filled membrane is supported on a powder-coated, 3 m (10 ft) high steel frame.

This pear-shaped work, exhibited at Le fort de Schoenenbourg in Hunspach, France, is a departure from earlier performance installations by Swiss artist Victorine Müller, who usually inhabits her giant, transparent, inflatable creations herself (pages 139 and 255). For *Erdling*, which means earthling, Müller suspended an inflatable ghost-like figure within a larger transparent bubble. A neon light added to the extraterrestrial effect. She says of her work: 'I'm interested in creating moments of sensitivity, moments when our defences are down and we are open to new things; moments of powerful concentration.'

Brazilian artist Geraldo Zamproni's massive pillow interventions have been exhibited across the globe. Each site placement established a tension between the puffed-up inflatables and the built environment in which they were located. The 6 x 6 m (20 x 20 ft) pillows, custom-made to encase existing columns, created the impression that they were supporting the weight of the structure overhead, establishing a surprising and delightful dialogue with the surrounding architecture. Here they are pictured at the Andalucía Museum of Memory as part of the 2012 Grenada Millennium Biennale in Spain.

Project name: **ADA**
Artist: **Karina Smigla-Bobinski**
Location: **São Paulo, Brazil** Date: **2011**

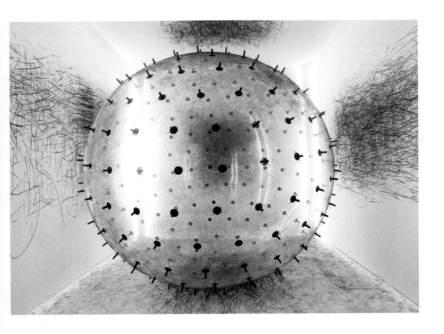

Exhibited in more than twenty countries, *ADA* was a transparent helium balloon measuring 1 m (3 ft) in diameter. Three hundred charcoal sticks were attached to its exterior at 25 cm (10 in) intervals. Once initiated, this interactive art-making 'machine' gained the momentum to create an indeterminate composition of lines and points. Visitors could observe or interact, but all attempts to control it were futile. Karina Smigla-Bobinski said, 'the blacker she [*ADA*] got from the charcoal and the more she was handled by visitors, the more she seemed to come alive.'

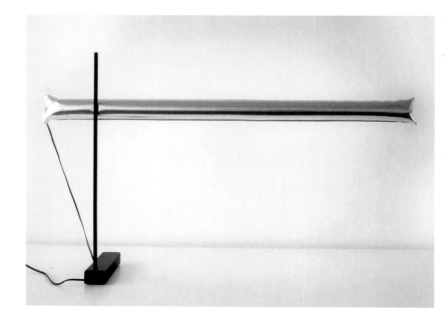

Arriving neatly packaged in a chrome can, the innovative Blow Me Up lamp is a plastic tube that is simply unrolled and inflated for use. With an integrated LED strip that illuminates from within, light is bounced off a reflective back panel and out through a translucent front strip, creating a subtle, diffused glow. Lightweight and portable, it is sturdy enough to simply lean against a wall to illuminate a space, or can be attached to the ceiling with fine nylon cords, creating the impression that they are floating.

Project name: **Ark Nova**
Architect/Artist: **Arata Isozaki and Anish Kapoor**
Location: **Matsushima, Japan (or elsewhere)** Date: **2013**

Created two years after a major earthquake and tsunami hit Japan in 2011, Ark Nova was intended to bring culture and spirit to communities still rebuilding after the devastation. Conceived by the architect and artist team of Arata Isozaki and Anish Kapoor as a travelling concert hall, the 30 m (110 ft) diameter, 18 m (60 ft) high, eggplant-hued, air-filled membrane could be transported to a venue, inflated, then deflated and folded, ready to travel to the next location. The uninterrupted internal space could accommodate five hundred people, and held events such as jazz concerts, performing arts shows and exhibitions.

Project name: **Moderna Museet Malmö**
Architect: **Plastique Fantastique**
Location: **Malmö, Sweden** Date: **2009**

Three months prior to the completion of the Moderna Museet Malmö in Sweden, the museum commissioned this large, white plastic pavilion to be installed in a street adjacent to the site. The structure swelled out from a tunnel attached to the unfinished building. Designed to promote the forthcoming opening of the museum, it was hoped that its unusual presence would spark public interest and increase membership. Refreshments were offered inside the space, as well as information on the new institution, accompanied by a video work, called *Speech Bubble*, by American artist Adam Leech.

Project name: **Inflatable Stool**
Designer/Architect: **Verner Panton and AMO**
Location: **Milan, Italy** Date: **2018**

Danish designer Verner Panton's 1961 inflatable stool displayed his customary flair for thinking in systems; the inflatable cubes could be used either individually or in sets to form flexible modules of sitting or reclining furniture. More recently AMO, the research studio of architecture firm OMA, used the transparent stool — an exclusive re-edition of the 1960s piece, produced by Verpan — for Prada's Spring/Summer 2019 Menswear show in Milan, Italy, creating an architectural field based on a cartesian framework. Numbers and symbols defined the exact positioning of the models in the space, alluding to geographic coordinates of remote places. Lit by purple-pink neons, the set had a Panton-esque, psychedelic edge.

The Blow Sofa forms part of a range of air-filled lounge chairs, which take the form of simple pillows. Extremely durable, the seats can withstand the pressure of two tonnes and collapse into a few flat elements for ease of transportation, assembly and reassembly. This first incarnation bears a similarity to oversized brown paper bags, made from 100% recyclable materials, tied together with rubber straps. Other collections have included a low-lying armchair available in more plush finishes, including wool covers and solid oak frame options with armrests.

Project name: **La Parole**
Artist: **Pablo Reinoso**
Location: **Various** Date: **1998**

Constructed from the same cloth as that used to make parachutes and hot-air balloons, *La Parole* features a pair of neck holes, one at each end, allowing two people to stick their heads inside. With the participants' bodies in view, the inflatable lozenge, which measured 6 m (20 ft) long, took on an alien-like appearance from the outside. Exploring a conceptual method by which humans could protect themselves from environmental pollution and other climatic conditions, it became a clean-air space in which to re-oxygenate. It also asked people to engage in a confined, potentially confronting and introspective space.

This travelling installation by Tokyo-based teamLab — an interdisciplinary collective that challenges the boundaries between art, science, technology and creativity — explored the idea that we are now so interconnected within the digital realm that each person, as a link in the global communication network, is able to transform the world in an instant. Visitors were immersed in a dream-like sea of giant, floating spheres, each of which contained data-collecting sensors. When touched, the orbs communicated with one another wirelessly, creating an environment in which the balloons, spreading the data to nearby balls, would become unified in colour.

Hussein Chalayan's Spring 2017 collection featured a series of puffed-up outfits in muted, earthy tones. The billowing silk balloon tops and dresses were tressed with flowing silk ribbons to create voluminous, otherworldly silhouettes. Rather than create this volume with an underlying structure, the forms were achieved by filling the garments with air. In his work, Chalayan eagerly embraces technology and the possibilities it creates for originality. 'I like technology because it's the only thing that allows you to do new things,' he says of the methods used to make this collection.

MAD Architects' temporary inflatable pavilion for Beijing Design Week 2017 was inspired by Lewis Carroll's *Alice In Wonderland*. The 6½ sq m (70 sq ft) wide, dome-shaped form was topped by two big floppy ears, thus resembling the white rabbit character from the novel. It was designed to provide a public space in a *hutong* — a narrow lane or alleyway in a traditional residential area of a Chinese city, especially Beijing — where children in the area could meet. After dark, the interior of the structure was illuminated with a bright white light that provided a safe environment for them to continue playing.

Israeli designer Tehila Guy wanted to design a chair that was lightweight and easily assembled at home, achieving the convenience of standard flat-pack furniture, but imbued with style. The resulting piece is made from a minimal wooden frame encased in transparent, inflatable cushions, with the playful appearance of invisibility. The cushions apply pressure to the branch-like rods, which keeps all the components together while, conversely, the frame helps support the form of the bubble-like cushions. Inspired by the blow-up furniture of the 1960s, Guy's chair calls to mind traditional pool-side outdoor furniture, with a twist.

Project name: **Park Bench Bubble**
Designer: **Thor ter Kulve**
Location: **London, England, UK** Date: **2014**

Park Bench Bubble is Thor ter Kulve's take on contemporary urban life. Based on insights from time spent in Amsterdam and London, his project creates a public–private space that transforms a modest timber park bench into a solo inflatable retreat with a solar-powered USB charger. Though hardly luxurious, the seat provides a place to work from, while the cocoon forms an opaque barrier that is embedded beneath the timber seat and accessed through a zipped entry. Fashioned from scavenged materials, the project strips back the idea of 'home' to the essentials: somewhere to power digital tools and protection against the elements.

Project name: **RedBall Project**
Artist: **Kurt Perschke**
Location: **Various** Date: **2001—ongoing**

Started in 2001, the ongoing *RedBall Project* is a globetrotting temporary art intervention. A huge red vinyl sphere measuring 4½ m (15 ft) in diameter and weighing 114 kg (250 lb), it is squeezed into unexpected, interstitial spaces including bridges, public squares and buildings. While undoubtedly playful, the ball also creates a sense of unease, squashed as it is into areas that appear too small. To date, *RedBall* has travelled through thirty cities, including Toronto, Paris and Sydney. A new site is chosen for the ball every day, with its installation in each place lasting between one and two weeks.

'I'd be smiling and chatting away and my mind would be floating around somewhere else, like a balloon with a broken string.' Haruki Murakami, *The Wind-Up Bird Chronicle*

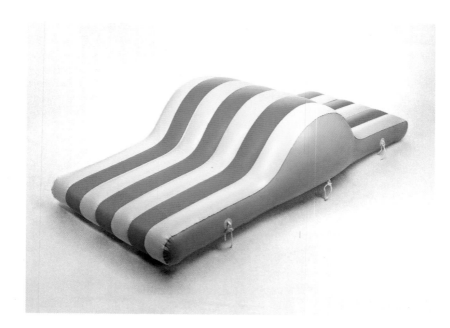

A cut above the ordinary pool bed, the Chat series by Spanish studio Imaisde consists of three striped inflatables in bold colours. Created to encourage interaction, each has six hooks and can be connected in forty-nine configurations, giving many possibilities for people to 'chat'. The designer describes their characters: 'Christina [above] lets you share your inflatable, while you read a book and your partner or friend is sun bathing with his feet in water. Henry [with a cushion at one end] is well thought through for sun bathing. Athina [with a cushion at either end] is perfect for having your feet up.'

Project name: **Rainbow City**
Artist: **Friends with You**
Location: **New York City, New York, USA** Date: **2011**

Rainbow City is a light-hearted assemblage of large-scale, candy-striped bubble forms and quirky characters that created a whimsical, playground-like environment. First exhibited in Toronto, Canada, then again for Art Basel, Miami, this interactive installation was latterly in New York for a month in celebration of the opening of the second section of the High Line, which has transformed a disused former railway line into a park and runs from W 20th to W 30th Street on Manhattan's West Side, through the Chelsea gallery district. The forty-piece installation occupied a 1500 sq m (16,000 sq ft) lot.

Project name: **Eden Project**
Architect: **Grimshaw Architects**
Location: **Bodelva, Cornwall, UK** Date: **2000**

The 'biomes' of the Eden Project, situated in Cornwall, in the southwest of England, were designed to be built upon the unstable ground of a former clay pit. Eight interlinked transparent geodesic domes cover over 2 ha (5½ ac) and contain thousands of plant species within simulated humid tropical and warm temperate climates. The extremely efficient, completely self-supporting structure of each dome is a hex-tri-hex space frame with triple-layer pillows of air-filled, environmentally efficient ETFE (ethylene tetrafluoroethylene) cladding panels. The panels vary in size up to 9 m (29½ ft) across, with the largest at the top of the structure.

Project name: **Beach Cocoon**
Designer: **Pascale de Backer**
Location: **Belgium** Date: **2017**

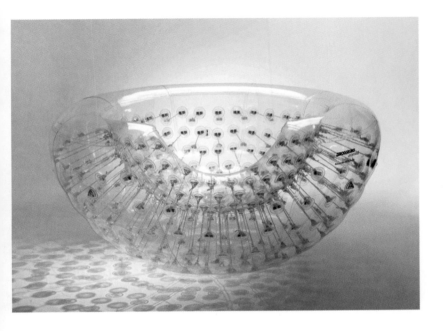

This pod-like, inflatable seat was created by Belgian designer Pascale de Backer to provide a versatile, comfortable, design-conscious beach chair that was easily portable, inflating in just five minutes. The Beach Cocoon is made from transparent PVC and features a blue dot detailing, evoking a jelly-like sea creature. Measuring 180 cm (71 in) in diameter and 90 cm (35 in) high, its curvaceous form is made to envelop and comfortably adapt to the body. The chair was displayed as part of a *SaloneSatellite* exhibition in Milan, Italy, in 2017, and is currently manufactured for commercial sale.

Project name: **With the Wind**
Architect: **Jiakun Architects**
Location: **Hong Kong** Date: **2002**

Installed in the northeast square of the Shenzhen Civic Centre as part of the Shenzhen Hong
Kong Biennale 2009, Liu Jiakun's whimsical sunshade pavilion appeared to hover in mid-air,
supported almost invisibly beneath fourteen large red spheres. Its undulating form gently
mimicked the enormous roofscape of the adjacent Civic Centre, the red inflatables setting up
a dialogue with its boldly colourful towers, while also gently supporting the suspended netting
that sheltered the space. Outdoor lounge and deck chairs beneath created a casual and
inclusive environment, offering respite from the hot days.

Project name: **Portavilion**
Architect: **Raumlabor**
Location: **London, England, UK** Date: **2010**

Created as part of the London Festival for Architecture, Raumlabor's inflatable Portavilion, nicknamed 'Rosy the Ballerina', was a translucent structure that hosted fifteen events in various parks and public spaces across London, England, UK, including productions by the English National Ballet (above) and an installation within Tate Modern. The pod-like form inflated rapidly out of the back of a vehicle and could easily be deflated and transported to its next location. The multi-bubble space could fit into courtyards, compress under bridges, wrap around trees, squeeze into corners or be blown up inside buildings.

This was one of a number of collaborative projects between sound and media artist Marco Barotti and Berlin-based group Plastique Fantastique, the latter specialising in creating temporary inflatable installations. Staged in Bern, Switzerland, this particular project, a contemporary dance piece, was produced with Swiss choreographer Anna Anderegg. Barotti created an evocative soundtrack that underpinned the work, which was played during and after the inflation of a number of large tubular bubbles. Four dancers then inhabited, interacted with, and emerged from within the network of translucent tubes, before disappearing into the nearby undergrowth.

Project name: **Spacebuster**
Architect: **Raumlabor**
Location: **New York City, New York, USA** Date: **2017**

Berlin-based architects Raumlabor's mobile, inflatable structure, Spacebuster, has been installed in various European locations since 2006. It emerges from its self-contained transportable compressor housing, the dome expanding organically to fill its surroundings. Here it was installed in collaboration with Storefront for Art and Architecture in New York City, New York, USA and was designed to explore the qualities and possibilities of public space. Made from durable translucent plastic, the 6 x 12 x 20 m (19½ x 39¼ x 65½ ft) pavilion provided a temporary location for community events including screenings, lectures and workshops for up to eighty people.

Project name: **Bulk Carrier**
Artist/Designer: **Norton Flavel**
Location: **Perth, Western Australia, Australia** Date: **2014**

This 8 m (26 ft) high inflatable was a super-scaled wine cask bag, an Australian invention that became part of popular culture (sometimes repurposed by children of the 1970s as camping pillows or pool toys). The reflective silver PVC outer convincingly replicated the thin metallic skin of a cask, despite being filled with air rather than wine. Located on the shifting sands of Cottesloe, a popular beach in Perth, *Bulk Carrier* was paradoxically both monolithic and ephemeral. The work, part of the Sculpture by the Sea festival, was a commentary on the excesses of consumerism, and queried the meaning and longevity of that materiality.

Project name: **Take My Hand, Rights and Weddings**
Designer: **Yael Reisner Studio**
Location: **Barcelona, Spain** Date: **2014**

In contrast to the historic surroundings of the Plaça de la Mercè, designer Yael Reisner's inflatable blue hand, referencing the universal symbol for human rights, was commissioned as part of the BCN re.set pavilion series in Barcelona, Spain. Extending over 20 m (65 ft) in length, the hand formed a vibrant canopy for civil wedding ceremonies that were celebrated beneath it — marking a change in Spanish law that legally recognized interfaith, non-religious and same-sex marriages. The PVC installation was suspended from adjacent buildings and secured by concrete weights, projecting a dramatic shadow that moved across the square throughout the day.

Project name: **Estar Azul**
Artist: **Penique Productions**
Location: **São Paulo, Brazil** Date: **2017**

This site-specific work, measuring 4 x 10 x 8 m (13 x 33 x 26 ft), was created for São Paulo Design Weekend in Brazil. Penique Productions coated a grand, domed domestic space — including furnishings — with a deep blue plastic membrane, unifying the room's elements and referencing an uninhabited underwater world to eerie effect. The work reflected on the future of our planet and the need for thoughtful, sustainable design. An inflatable remote-controlled shark 'swam' gracefully through the space, providing a sense of menace, and highlighted the need for us to take care of its environment.

Project name: **Inflatable Jacket**
Designer: **Balenciaga**
Location: **Paris, France** Date: **2017**

This oversized, marigold yellow inflatable vest, a reworked version of Balenciaga's cult puffer jacket, was part of the label's Spring 2017 collection, designed by Demna Gvasalia. Comprising a quilted waterproof shell with front pockets, snap fastenings and two valves, one at the neck and one at the waist, which can be used to adjust its volume, the piece more than closely resembles a life vest and carries a price tag of £1,595. While it may look the part, the fashion house advises that it is for 'urban use only'.

Designer Nick Crosbie first worked with inflatables at college, experimenting with scraps of PVC and a welder to make a blow-up fruit bowl. His Antwerp-based studio, Inflate, established in 1995, has since expanded to include the design and production of inflatable structures, furniture, lights and home accessories, including bowls, egg cups and vases. The bold form of this chair consists of seven glossy, white individual pillows, supported by a gently curving tubular steel frame. Its simple, minimal shape gives the chair a floating appearance and an elegant edge.

Bertjan Pot produced these lamps using a technique he had experimented with a decade earlier. At that time, he worked with knitted fabric to shape a form around a cluster of balloons, leaving a hollow space within. In this iteration, however, he used a homemade laminate of glass fibre mats, some textiles and metallic-coloured wrapping paper (gift wrap). The balloons are sealed within the skin, forming a large, lumpy, whimsical pendant. Only minimally translucent but with a bright golden interior that serves as an effective reflector, the lamps emit an intense warm glow.

Project name: **Inflato Dumpster**
Architect: **John Locke and Joaquin Reyes**
Location: **New York City, New York, USA** Date: **2016**

This inflatable classroom installed inside a dumpster functioned as a mobile learning laboratory in a residential area of Manhattan, New York. The workshops, documentary screenings and musical performances conducted here pushed the boundaries of traditional formats for theatres and classrooms. During the project's three-day lifespan, more than five hundred people in the neighbourhood interacted with the installation. Weighing less than 9 kg (20 lb), the skin was made from inexpensive clear polyethylene, which allowed views in and out of the space, interspersed with Mylar panels that added a metallic luminosity.

Project name: **Opblæst Ring and Puffed Up Pendants**
Designer: **Kim Buck**
Location: **Copenhagen, Denmark** Date: **Various**

A goldsmith by trade, Danish jewellery designer Kim Buck's range of gold inflatable pieces provides a commentary on the perception of value within the jewellery industry. The simple, elegant, wearable pieces are crafted from thin gold sheet that has been welded and filled with air, embodying the lustre of more traditional jewels, but without the literal and figurative weight. The Opblæst collection includes rings that riff on the conventional diamond shape (above), while the Puffed Up series features O- and bell-shaped pendants (opposite). A series of heart-shaped brooches utilize metalized plastic foil.

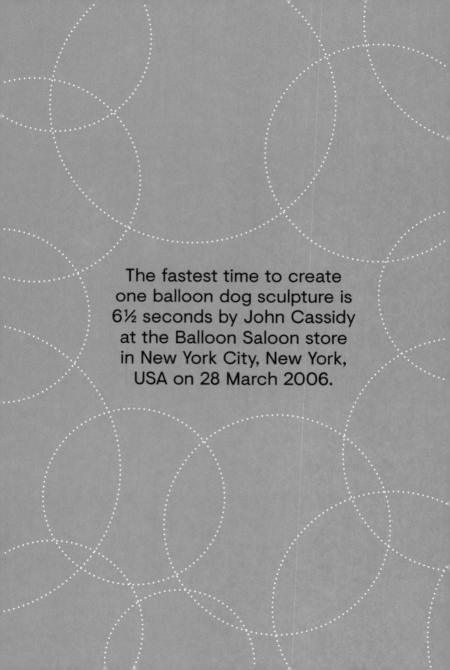

The fastest time to create
one balloon dog sculpture is
6½ seconds by John Cassidy
at the Balloon Saloon store
in New York City, New York,
USA on 28 March 2006.

Project name: **Big Blo 2-Seater**
Designer: **Blofield**
Location: **Amsterdam, The Netherlands** Date: **2013**

The Blofield company focuses on producing playful inflatable furniture and this, the Big Blo sofa — a witty spin on the traditional leather Chesterfield — is lightweight and weatherproof, featuring the classic rolled arms and deep buttoned back tufting of the original design. Constructed from robust UV-proof PVC, with additional reinforcement on the base, the Big Blo 2-Seater can be used both indoor and out. The range comes in white, red and black, and consists of single, two-seater, four-seater and child-sized versions, all of which can be inflated and deflated within minutes.

Project name: **Almost Nothing**
Artist: **Clive Murphy**
Location: **Minneapolis, Minnesota, USA** Date: **2011**

This inflatable grid-work was a site-specific installation in a warehouse space in Minneapolis in Minnesota, USA. In line with Murphy's propensity for working with lo-fi technology, it was made from bin (garbage) bags filled with air by electric fans. Murphy has stated that he is interested in exploring 'the peripheral, insignificant and seemingly ridiculous as a means of illustrating a sense of interconnectivity and also rebutting certain hierarchical value systems'. Here, he created a series of room-like non-rooms that had the presence of architectural space and form while being made of 'almost nothing'.

This midas-hued, helium-filled structure was part of an exhibition at the Museum of Contemporary Art (MOT) in Tokyo, Japan, which explored the possibilities of new spatial practices for architectural environments of the future. Developed as a prototype (this is a 1:5 scale model) of a larger outdoor version, it appeared to levitate in the gallery space. amid.cero9, a collaboration between Cristina Díaz Moreno and Efrén García Grinda, designed The Golden Balloon's form with welding points, seams, anchoring points and holes that allowed it to adapt to the topography, so it could provide emergency shelter in a crisis.

Project name: **Momo at the Souks**
Artist: **Penique Productions**
Location: **Beirut, Lebanon** Date: **2013**

Set in a terraced garden of citrus trees and vibrant climbing Bougainvillea plants, this Moroccan restaurant, Momo at the Souks, was completely transformed for a week during the annual Beirut Art Fair in Lebanon. The intervention was typical of the work of Spanish art collective Penique Productions, in which a huge blow-up membrane was inflated to entirely cover the periphery of the room, so as to highlight architectural details. As the restaurant continued to trade, the furniture and other practical items were reinstalled within the all-white space, creating a playful, surreal dining experience.

Project name: **Wine Rack and Star Vase**
Designer: **Inflate**
Location: **London, England, UK** Date: **1997**

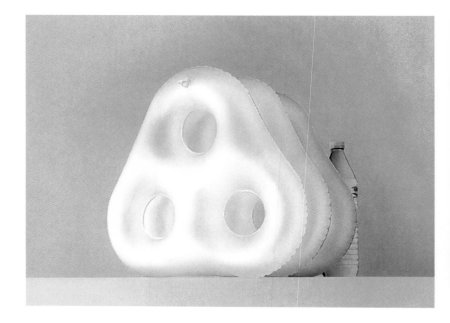

Inflate studio's range of small-scale, blow-up products was designed between 1995 and 2000. Items included a vase (opposite), fruit bowl, mirrors and wine rack (above). The business arose almost accidentally when founder Nick Crosbie began experimenting with some scrap PVC for a college project. He inserted a valve and inflated the piece which, fortuitously, resembled a fruit bowl. He set up Inflate with partners Mike and Mark Sodeau and evolved the bowl, alongside other fun, functional and affordable products, into marketable items.

At the forefront of inflatable design in the 1960s, the Blow Chair was the first piece of furniture that used air as its structural framework. Considered one of the most important pieces of the 'pop' design movement, it created a new paradigm for furniture and quickly became a bestseller. Although no longer in production, versions of the transparent PVC lounger are housed in design collections around the world, including the Museum of Modern Art in New York, the New Collection in Munich, the Vitra Design Museum in Weil am Rhein, Germany and the Victoria and Albert Museum in London.

Project name: **Pavillon Martell de SelgasCano**
Architect: **SelgasCano**
Location: **Cognac, France** Date: **2017**

This undulating, snake-like pavilion filled the vast courtyard of Fondation d'Entreprise Martell
in Cognac, France. Yellow inflatable seats were strapped onto the main structure, constructed
from transparent onduline — a recycled cellulose fibre that is saturated with bitumen under
intense pressure and heated to create a strong 1 mm (0.03 in) thick continuous membrane
that resembles rice paper. Integral to both the function and aesthetic of the pavilion, the chairs
allowed visitors to sit or recline. With an events programme that promoted collaborations, the
structure was commissioned to occupy the space into which the building will eventually expand.

Project name: **Sound of Light**
Architect: **Marco Barotti and Plastique Fantastique**
Location: **Hamm, Germany** Date: **2014**

This site-specific installation was set within the portico of a music pavilion as part of the
Urban Lights Ruhr festival in Hamm, Germany. A camera mounted on the top of the inflatable
structure filmed the sky, dividing it into six parts: RGB and CMY. The six colours were filtered
into six corresponding columns within the structure (right). The screen colours (red, green,
blue) and print colours (cyan, magenta, yellow, minus black) were dynamically transformed
into audio frequencies. Each colour was assigned different oscillations, converting them from
visible to audible via a series of woofers fixed onto the bottom of each inflatable.

Christo's *Big Air Package* was the largest ever inflated envelope without a skeleton. It was installed inside the Gasometer Oberhausen, Germany, one of the largest gas tanks in the world. At 90 m (295 ft) high and 50 m (164 ft) wide, the cylinder-shaped balloon was gargantuan, nearly spanning the wall-to-wall distance of the tank. Two fans were used to keep the package pressurized with a volume of 177,000 cubic m (6,250,000 cubic ft) of air. Illuminated through the skylights of the Gasometer, the work was a cathedral of air, with an atmosphere of silence and tranquillity.

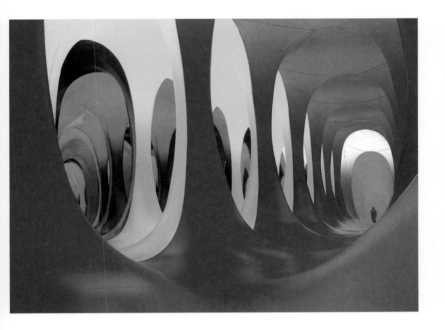

Artist Maurice Agis' inflatable installations date back to the mid-1960s. The first *Dreamspace*, a series of huge interactive inflatables, was commissioned in 1996, and many followed. Designed as a holistic sensory experience for the participant, immersed in vibrant colours and psychedelic sounds, *Dreamspaces* were air-filled mazes of pods with different colours that played off the special cape visitors were given to wear at the entrance. Unfortunately, forty years of public art practice by Agis was overshadowed when *Dreamspace V* came adrift from its moorings with thirty people inside, killing two and leaving thirteen injured.

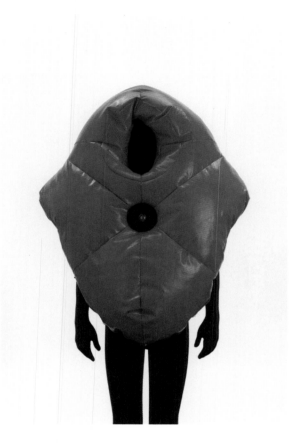

Suited for Subversion was a conceptual prototype for a contemporary suit of armour, designed to be worn by street protesters as protection from police batons. South African designer Ralph Borland developed the suit as a consequence of time spent as an activist in New York City. A video camera mounted over the wearer's head recorded police action, and a speaker in the centre of the suit amplified the heartbeat, creating a natural soundtrack that was audible across crowds as tension and excitement built.

Project name: **Roomograph**
Artist: **Alex Schweder**
Location: **Lincoln, Massachusetts, USA** Date: **2011**

This installation, exhibited at deCordova Sculpture Park and Museum in Lincoln, Massachusetts featured two rooms zipped together, which inflated and deflated in the dark, pushing each other out of the way like a pop-up book as they morphed. When the inflatables were in their stable position, visitors could occupy *Roomograph* with the lights on. The inhabitable areas were lined with white fur that glowed in the dark when the lights were out. A photosensitive treatment of the surfaces left an impression where people sat or reclined, blocking the light from the lining. This created slowly transitioning silhouettes that were subsequently replaced by imprints of fresh interactions.

This site-specific installation was created for Festival IN, an innovation and creativity fair, in Lisbon, Portugal. The project was named after the 180 cm (6 ft) grid around which the work was based. A series of 8 m (26¼ ft) high flagpoles determined the positioning of the huge red inflatable that wove its way through them. The work was designed to be experienced from two perspectives: the open-air space within the structure, defined by the external form, and inside the inflatable itself. The white flagpoles and vibrantly coloured membrane stood in contrast to the serene, dream-like space within.

First commissioned for the Art en Plein air festival in Môtier, Switzerland, artist Victorine Müller's *Le Moment Végétatif* showed the artist, strikingly dressed in hot pink, contained within a transparent inflatable structure. The abstract, organic form twisted and wound into the tree canopy above, merging with the branches and leaves. Müller's evocative performance installations always seek to question the representation and materiality of the body: physical, spiritual or energetic. This work, which was more than 9 m (29½ ft) high, was later shown in 2010 as part of the Festival Arbres en Lumières in Geneva, Switzerland.

Designed by Phillip Schöne and Emma Penttinen for Essex County Council, this nylon folly was a response to a commission for an interactive arts project for The People Speak collective, with assistance from Inflate. Its swollen body creates a distinctive pavilion for the housing estate in which it stands, giving local residents an easily-assembled place for many different users to meet. Punctuated by three different openings and animated by colourful Perspex windows, Inflatable Space was developed through a process of public consultation; its bulbous body evokes the visual language of insects — bugs and butterflies being especially popular with local children.

The form of Kengo Kuma & Associates' modern Tee Haus, installed at the Museum of Applied Art in Frankfurt during the summer, eschewed traditional structures and materials such as wood, bamboo and paper. In contrast, it was created using a double-layered membrane of Tenara, a high-tech fabric that can expand and contract when inflated. The membranes were tied together with polyester string at 60 cm (23½ in) intervals, connecting the inflatable layers and creating a texture of points inside and out, like a quilted igloo. At night, the almost translucent skins glowed from within.

'Inflatables are big, cheap, easy to make and transform life into this magic bubble.'
Mary Hale

Crafted from fine metalized polyester, Basic Home swiftly transforms from golden square to quirky, blow-up pad. This super lightweight accommodation is activated by heat from sun or bodies, the cubic form expanding to create a shelter for two people, and deflating to fit into the back pocket of a pair of trousers. Coated with gold on one side and silver on the other, the cosy, low-impact shelter provides protection from both heat and cold. This makes Basic Home useful for post-disaster applications; it occupies very little space, but gives a lot back.

Project name: **Allianz Arena**
Architect: **Herzog & de Meuron**
Location: **Munich, Germany** Date: **2005**

Conceived as a luminous body in the open landscape, this Munich-based football stadium
can continuously change in appearance using LED lights to suit particular themes, heralding its
presence to approaching fans. With a capacity of close to 70,000, the footprint is 37,600
sq m (404,723 sq ft). The translucent skin of the shell is composed of more than 4,000 diamond-
shaped ETFE (ethylene tetrafluoroethylene) inflated cushions, each of which is digitally controlled
to illuminate separately in white, red or blue, or any combination of these.

Originally intended to be used over multiple floors, this bridge was a prototype for an inflatable building system. Spanning a 6 m (20 ft) wide watercourse, this test pilot was installed in artist and designer Lambert Kamps' hometown of Groningen, The Netherlands. The construction consisted of only pressurized air and cloth, and its walls were strengthened with the lateral support provided by the grid of portholes. As a prototype to test the viability and possibilities of inflatable spans, it proved successful, however the envisioned building did not proceed.

Project name: **Leviathan**
Artist: **Anish Kapoor**
Location: **Paris, France** Date: **2011**

With its dark red membrane and translucent red interior, *Leviathan* was a triadic form of 35 m
(115 ft) high interconnected spheres, with a central joining chamber which could be entered.
Erected as a site-specific installation for the nave of the Grand Palais in Paris, there was a
cathedral-like scale to the sculpture's volume that imbued a sense of awe and contemplation.
Exploring relationships between memory and the body, inside *Leviathan* you were at once
reminded of both an organic outer space and an inner corporeal self.

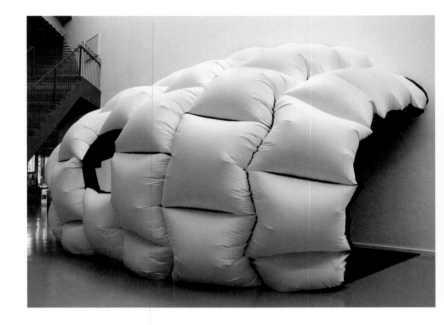

Conceived by artist and designer Lambert Kamps, this pod was formed of tightly connected, inflated pillows that created an intimate space to be used for projections in both indoor and outdoor locations. The variation in pillow size permitted a natural arch to form, so that the structure could be leaned against a wall; an absent pillow created a window that allowed a passing glimpse of the activity within. It was installed as one of a series of similar installations within the Centre for Visual Arts in Groningen, The Netherlands.

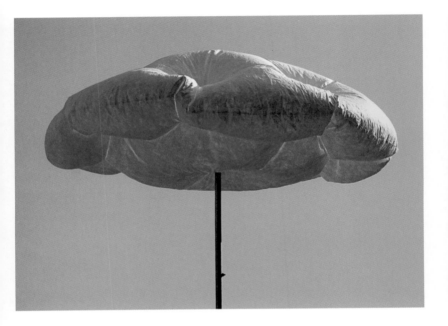

This whimsical, solar-powered parasol self-inflates to a diameter of 2 m (6½ ft) in 20 seconds when the sun starts shining. Constructed of silicone-coated white nylon, it does not have an internal metal frame like a conventional parasol, making it lightweight and durable; it is also waterproof and aerodynamic. Solar panels positioned on the top power a small fan that keeps it inflated. When the sun goes away, the Cumulus automatically deflates, or it can be turned off manually via a switch on the pole.

Project name: **Stuffed Full**
Artist: **Jimmy Kuehnle**
Location: **Kyoto, Japan** Date: **2008**

American artist Jimmy Kuehnle crammed eighteen voluminous red inflatable tubes into the front of a small gallery space in Kyoto, Japan for this playful installation. Created as a smaller version of a previous work, each extrusion had a diameter of 55 cm (21½ in) and measured 5 m (16½ ft) long. The resulting work had a humorous edge, but also questioned architectural space by altering perceptions of function and scale. The effect was inverted and amplified at night, as the cylinders, illuminated by the light emanating from the gallery behind, appeared to be vying to escape.

Project name: **Guidepost to the Eternal Space**
Artist: **Yayoi Kusama**
Location: **Moscow, Russia** Date: **2015**

Recreating the hallucinatory patterns Yayoi Kusama experienced as a child, her 1965 installation *Infinity Mirror Room — Phalli's Field* was the first to combine the polka dots and mirrors that would become her trademark motifs. The works can be seen as a means of confronting her childhood fears by representing them on a grand scale, an approach she described as 'self-obliteration'. *Guidepost to the Eternal Space* — here displayed at the Garage Museum of Contemporary Art in Moscow, Russia — furthers this intent with the creation of saturated environments that include large-scale inflatables of various organic, spherical forms. With these tools, the artist constructs bewildering spaces through the consideration of form, pattern, light and colour.

Project name: **Drift**
Designer: **Snarkitecture**
Location: **Miami, Florida, USA** Date: **2012**

Creating a dreamy entry to the main pavilion for DesignMiami/ in Florida, USA, this installation by Snarkitecture played with the vernacular of the vinyl event tent, reconfiguring the material to form a transitional zone that encouraged guests to linger and mingle. Slivers of soft light permeated the space through crevices and voids in the overhead canopy. The tube formation undulated to resemble a topographical landscape — a mountain range above and a cavern of stalactites below — with the sheer scale of the installation being countered by the lightness of the inflated tubes.

Inspired by the Japanese tradition of *Hanami*, which celebrates the ephemeral beauty of cherry blossoms, this installation — part of the Lively Architecture Festival in Montpellier, France — was installed within the courtyard of a hotel, employing hundreds of pink and white balloons. Suspended on a mesh netting over the atrium, 650 balloons were dispersed each day, allowing viewers to immerse themselves in 'petals' as they floated down to the grassy square below. More than 4,000 balloons were used over the duration of the installation.

Project name: **Creature Craft**
Designer: **Darren Vancil**
Location: **Grand Junction, Colorado, USA** Date: **1997**

A new generation of white-water inflatable, the Creature Craft's patented roll cage restricts the boat from settling upside down in the water and protects users within from rocks and other potential hazards. The principal innovation of these rafts is the self-righting system, which helps prevent capsizing while keeping the users seated inside, securely strapped in with a lap belt, and able to reposition themselves. The Creature Craft also accelerates the learning curve of tackling rapid runs by keeping you in the raft. Creator Darren Vancil was inspired after watching videos of Russian white-water enthusiasts navigating Siberian Rivers in hand-built rafts called 'Bublik'.

Project name: **Traft**
Designer: **Traft**
Location: **Utah, USA** Date: **2017**

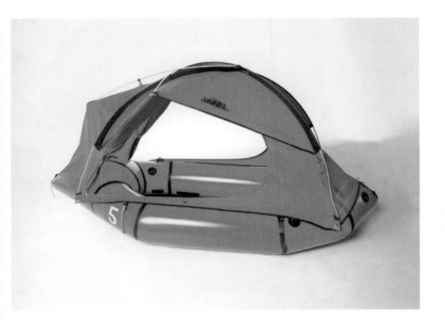

As the name suggests, this hybrid craft combines a boat with a place to sleep, delivering a new way to adventure travel. The two components of the Traft are usable separately: as a raft with detachable shade shelter and as a tent for camping, with a flip of the boat providing an instant blow-up bed. Easily transported, it inflates almost instantly and, once deflated, can be packed down into a backpack. The Traft is made of TPU (thermoplastic polyurethane), an ultra-durable, lightweight, abrasion-resistant material that contains no toxic chemicals and is one hundred per cent recyclable.

Nike's Flyknit technology is employed to create these inflatable seats with brightly coloured, woven skins. Inspired by the clever simplicity of William H Miller's 1944 Chair — which placed a car tyre inner tube on four legs — Bertjan Pot utilizes the tubes of a car, a wheelbarrow, a truck and a tractor as structural framework. Pot's work plays with the dichotomy of rest and activity, and the use of tyres furthers the conceptual contradiction of movement and repose. With an overlay of structures, patterns and colours, there is a distinct interplay between high-tech materials and traditional techniques.

Project name: **Microcity Sales Office**
Architect: **Mossine Partners**
Location: **Moscow, Russia** Date: **2013**

This temporary inflatable office sat — either starkly or almost camouflaged, depending on the season — within an open landscape outside Moscow, Russia, resembling an enormous igloo or a futuristic movie set. With 1,400 sq m (15,000 sq ft) of internal space, it was constructed as a showroom for the real-estate company developing the surrounding site. Three conjoined bubbles housed the exhibition space, a sales area, a café and children's play zone. The facade system was constructed of a membrane of PVC fabric with vertical facets that divided the domes into a series of undulating balloon forms.

Project name: **SiloSilo**
Architect: **Plastique Fantastique**
Location: **Pilsen, Czech Republic** Date: **2016**

Exploring the sustainable use of plastic in everyday life, the *SiloSilo* exhibition consisted of an assemblage of cylindrical inflatable tubes of various sizes, each made from different recycled materials that hosted video projections, PET installations and conference spaces. The exhibition sought to bring awareness to recycling and upcycling possibilities. As a precursor to the show, Berlin-based Plastique Fantastique installed a doughnut-shaped inflatable structure (above) in the centre of Pilsen, Czech Republic, the volume of which was equivalent to the amount of plastic waste produced by the city in a three-day period.

Project name: **Luci**
Designer: **MPOWERD**
Location: **USA** Date: **2012**

This inflatable solar lantern, called Luci, was conceived to provide simple, affordable access to light for millions in the developing world who were without electricity. Its secondary purpose is as a clean energy product for camping or outdoor events. The lightweight LED is ultra-compact, waterproof and solar-powered and can function as a task light, torch (flashlight) or emergency beacon. Various models are available, weighing from 156 g (5½ oz) to the lightest at 72 g (2½ oz); they are collapsible down to 2½ cm (1 in). The Luci can provide illumination for up to fifty hours from a single charge.

The work of Dutch collective Spatial Effects, a company specializing in creating memorable inflatables, these unusual structures allowed people to walk on water in an over-scaled, largely transparent cube. The first realization of a water leisure vehicle was in the shape of a tetrahedron, created in 1969 (top right); a tubular version, called Waterwalk 2 (bottom right), followed in 1975. Decades later in 2005, the orange version (above) was made. Strong enough to contain several people, this latter iteration of Waterwalk was formed of heavy gauge PVC filled with air, creating a lightweight, breathable space, ready to roll.

The largest inflatable beach ball is 19.97 m (65 ft 6 in) in diameter and was created for the *Baywatch* film in London, England, UK on 31 May 2017.

Inflate's Office in a Bucket was created in response to a request for a pop-up breakout space. The lightweight structure inflates from a conveniently portable plastic container into a versatile room in less than five minutes, and can serve variably as an exhibition or meeting space, a private retreat or a chill-out pod; the structure can be closed with a simple clip fastener for privacy. In the base of the bucket, a low noise emission fan system keeps the room inflated when plugged into a power source.

Designed to accommodate two wide-body aircraft, such as a Boeing 707, side by side, this hangar is the largest inflatable structure in the world to date. Installed in Getafe, Spain, it measures 54 m (177 ft) wide and 23 m (75½ ft) high. Originally built 75 m (246 ft) in length, the hangar was extended to 110 m (360 ft) two years later. The lightweight nature of the building means that it can be delivered in six months, requiring no conventional foundations. Easy deployment on unprepared terrains means the Hangar H54 model could prove invaluable for emergency operations.

Project name: **Tight Spot**
Artist: **David Byrne**
Location: **New York City, New York, USA** Date: **2011**

Former Talking Head's front man, David Byrne, created this installation within a space acquired by the Pace Gallery. The 15 x 6 m (48 x 20 ft) inflatable globe, based on those used for teaching in schools, was enlarged and wedged within the space beneath New York's High Line, becoming distorted in the process. A low-frequency vibration emanated from speakers within it, attracting the attention of passers by. Byrne imagined the map as: 'a wholly unrealistic world, a world of somewhat arbitrary political units, not a planet of clouds, deep blue oceans, beige deserts and swaths of green jungle.'

Project name: **Project Loon**
Designer: **Google**
Location: **USA** Date: **2016**

Using super-sized helium-filled balloons, Google have embarked on a project to deliver Internet access to over half the world's population that currently does not have it. Project Loon has taken the vital components of a telecommunications tower and redesigned them to be light and durable, able to withstand winds of more than 100 km (62 mi) per hour and temperatures as low as minus 90 degrees Celsius (194 degrees Farenheit). Travelling at 20 km (12 mi) per hour, the 15 m (49¼ ft) diameter polyethylene balloons carry remote-controlled, solar-powered electronics systems that beam down high-speed cellular Internet coverage.

Project name: **Itinerant Home**
Architect: **Mary Hale**
Location: **New Orleans, Louisiana, USA** Date: **2010**

Five years after New Orleans was devastated by Hurricane Katrina, the local Chapter of the American Institute of Architects commissioned architect, educator and artist Mary Hale to create an interactive multi-purpose work in response to the ongoing effort of rebuilding the city. With the main structure being made of breathable ripstop nylon with a black vinyl floor, this wearable, inflatable house had the capacity to shelter multiple people as they worked together, navigating historic neighbourhoods and waterways. In spite of its apparent fun nature, Itinerant Home was a catalyst for discussion of different housing models.

This zany, multi-armed inflatable suit is the work of performance artist Jimmy Kuehnle, who has made numerous appearances wearing it in various cities across the United States. The multi-hued inflatable costume features an array of purple, pink and orange dangling appendages, attached like centipede legs, and inflated with the help of a portable battery pack. The suit has been viewed as akin to battalion armour, allowing Kuehnle a sense of enclosure and disguise. Despite its protuberant form, he claims to be able to 'run as fast as anything' in it.

Project name: **Apollo Chair**
Designer: **Quasar Khanh**
Location: **Paris, France** Date: **1968**

A pioneer in the creation of inflatable seating, Paris-based Vietnamese inventor Quasar Khanh revolutionized furniture design in the 1960s. The release of his Aerospace collection, the world's first-ever line of inflatable furniture, propelled him to the status of pop-culture icon by the end of the decade. The range included the Apollo chair (above), Chesterfield sofa (opposite) and Relax lounge chair, as well as a selection of inflatable lamps. Pieces were crafted by hand in the suburbs of Paris between 1968 and 1972 in a factory that also produced pool toys. In 1969 these PVC icons were exhibited at the Musée des Arts Décoratifs in Paris and the Triennale Design Museum in Milan.

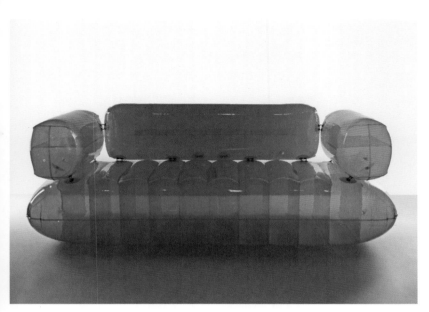

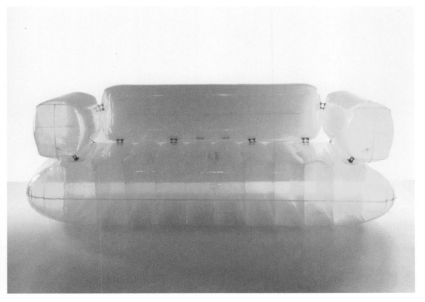

Project name: **Inflatable RGBubble**
Designer: **Pneuhaus**
Location: **Rumford, Rhode Island, USA** Date: **2015**

This tri-partite inflatable pod, in which red, green and blue domes intersected, placed visitors within the RGB colour spectrum. Light rays entered through a small central void — in addition to the general translucence of the coloured fabric — and combined inside the structure to project the entire visible spectrum across the white floor. The RGBubble allowed visitors to understand light interactions that are part of everyday life, while also offering a serene space in which to relax. The pod was installed at Brown University as part of A Better World by Design conference in Rhode Island, USA.

This extraterrestrialesque, temporary pavilion was created for Dialog:City, an arts and cultural event in Denver, Colorado, USA. Inflated by blowers at the base of its thirty-five columns, the 56¼ m (185 ft) long, 25 m (82 ft) wide pneumatic structure absorbed passing wind currents to maintain its 4 m (13 ft) high array of nine hexagonal canopies. The nylon fabric was coated with a gradient of reflective silver dots that mirrored its surroundings, casting playful shadow patterns and emanating an iridescent speckled glow when illuminated at night.

Artist Hans Hemmert's large-scale, soft yellow balloon works are amorphous and inanimate, yet at the same time disarmingly lifelike and endearing. His work references the vulnerability between the individual and their surroundings. Squeezing his human-scale balloons into the architecture of the space that they inhabit, they deform and bulge, creating a relationship between the two. Here, a balloon is displayed at the Galicia Contemporary Arts Centre in Spain; in other iterations, the balloon works playfully engage with objects in daily gestures, such as hugging a friend, holding a baby, riding a motor-scooter and drinking a beer.

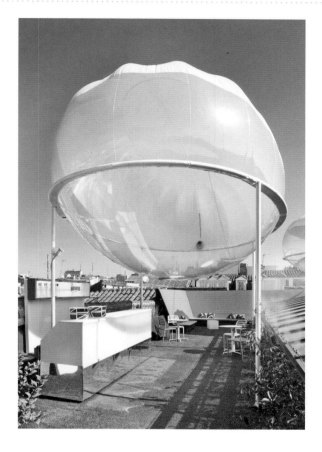

Sited on a narrow, U-shaped rooftop bar in the centre of Madrid, Spain, the Clouds Observatory
is an experimental, low-energy alternative to air-conditioning. Consisting of three spherical
inflatable pods made from lightweight white and transparent plastic sheeting, they are supported
by a simple steel structure. The architect's intention was for vaporization beneath the canopies to
form denser and fresher air; unlike air conditioning, which cools a space by heating an adjoining
one, the energy embedded in vapour particles in this system migrates to upper layers of the
atmosphere, decreasing the warming of the soil and building materials.

Japanese fashion designer Naoki Takizawa's presentation for Issey Miyake's Spring/Summer 2000 Ready-to-Wear collection, shown at the École des Beaux-Arts in Paris, France, featured this bulbous grey inflatable dress, its oversized pea-shaped form disguising the shape of the model's body. Takizawa went on to create inflatable breeches for his Spring/Summer 2001 collection, a satirical nod to the padding traditionally used in trousers to enhance aspects of the masculine body.

The Serpentine Pavilion, an annual commission for a temporary pavilion by a high-profile architect who has not previously had a built work in Britain, was co-designed by architect Rem Koolhaas and structural designer Cecil Balmond in 2006. The design consisted of a large ovoid inflatable canopy poised over a circular enclosure. Located in London's Hyde Park, the pavilion served as a café and forum for televised public programmes, live talks and film screenings. Fabricated from translucent material, the structure was illuminated from within at night, acting as a beacon above the gallery's lawn.

Project name: **RINGdeLUXE**
Architect: **Plastique Fantastique**
Location: **Neukölln, Germany** Date: **2011**

This installation, RINGdeLUXE, by Berlin-based collective Plastique Fantastique, was created for the 48 Hours Neukölln art festival near Templhof, Germany. The shiny inflatable gold ring hugged an archway and acted as a beacon to highlight the entrance to the festival. The lightweight, over-scaled structure made a conceptual link between the connection of people to architecture and the public domain, while posing questions of its own verisimilitude. The ring has also been displayed in Logroño, Spain, hooked around the tower of a historic building, as part of Concéntrico, an international festival of architecture and design.

Project name: **Au premier matin**
Artist: **Klaus Pinter**
Location: **Chaumont-sur-Loire, France** Date: **2013**

Austrian artist Klaus Pinter was a founding member of the seminal Haus-Rucker-Co collective, which originated in Vienna in 1967 (page 249). His pneumatic structure *Au premier matin* — an enormous PVC ball clad in golden flowers — was wedged into an archway of the stables at the Centre d'Arts et de Nature de Chaumont sur Loire in France. Pinter's 8 m (26¼ ft) diameter sphere is reminiscent of the decorative dome that crowns the Secession Building in Vienna, Austria, which features an inscription over its entrance that Pinter says could be his own motto: 'To every age its art. To every art its freedom.'

Drawing on the work of inflatable pioneers Jeffrey Shaw, of Spatial Effects (page 162), and the Ant Farm collective (page 223), this Antepavilion project — a commission for a floating structure to be sited on the Regent's Canal at Hoxton Docks in Hackney, London — was designed by local architects Thomas Randall-Page and Benedetta Rogers. Conceived as a grass-roots arts venue, the bright yellow bubble was set atop a steel barge. When inflated from below, a robust tethered membrane produced a soft, playful landscape for lounging around on, while above, a lighter membrane provided shelter and enclosure. Able to inflate in twelve minutes and deflate in five, the pop-up space manoeuvred easily under low-level bridges along London's canal network.

Project name: **String Vienna**
Designer: **Numen/For Use**
Location: **Vienna, Austria** Date: **2014**

String Prototype was an evolution of net-based and inflatable art installations by Numen/For Use. Inspired by the structure and form of inflatable advertising cubes, the designers created this super-sized version with an internal space large enough for visitors to move within, allowing them to monkey around on a gridded matrix of ropes. The ropes were connected to the interior walls and engineered to create the cubic shape with no additional structure. Inflated until the outer skin had enough tension to stretch the strings within, the structure formed a very cool, architectural climbing gym for anyone game to give it a go.

Project name: **The Cloud**
Designer: **Phillipe Starck**
Location: **Montpellier, France** Date: **2015**

Phillipe Starck's distinctive building was designed as a 3,000 sq m (32,300 sq ft) health and wellness facility in Montpellier, that includes a gym, swimming pool, café, children's play area, hairdressers and salon. The first inflatable private building in France, it utilizes lightweight, air-filled ETFE (ethylene tetrafluoroethylene) panels that have integrated lighting, allowing the building to change colour. Starck describes Le Nuage, which means The Cloud, as 'the opposite of an architectural gesture. It is a "nearly nothing"; an urban space ... a magic bubble that is virtually indestructible, even though it only has the thickness of a few tenths of a millimetre.'

'Nobody can be
uncheered with a balloon.'
AA Milne, *Winnie the Pooh*

Project name: **BuBble**
Architect/Artist: **Studio MMASA with Cipriano Chas**
Location: **Mexico (or elsewhere)** Date: **2009**

Designed by Patricia Muñiz and Luciano G Alfaya, with Cipriano Chas, the BuBble was envisaged as a temporary form of accommodation for transient people or those displaced from their homes. Enclosed by four walls of inflated transparent plastic, the nomadic skinned structure is supported by a demountable tubular aluminium frame, with an operable wall/door that hinges open to allow entry, as well as creating a protective canopy. In order to meet the minimum needs for human hygiene and comfort, the BuBble also includes a water point and single gas hob. The entire unit — including cooking equipment and folding camping stool — packs down into a single box.

Project name: **Snoozy**
Designer: **Inflate and Airclad**
Location: **London, England, UK** Date: **2013**

The Snoozy was first conceived as a portable accommodation solution for outdoor, multi-day festivals. A flat-packed sleeping unit for two to four people, the extruded aluminium frame is assembled in minutes then wrapped in a double-layer membrane into which air is pumped. The Airclad pneumatic system also solves the need for a lightweight insulating skin to keep the interior warm. A series of products have since been developed, including a smaller model that can be packed into a duffle bag, and a larger villa model complete with en suite.

Originally conceived as a response to mobility issues — old age, sickness, handicap or temporary immobilization — this remote-controlled inflatable booster seat-cum-pillow allows the chest or legs to be raised with no effort. Designed by Bina Baitel in conjunction with textile designer Luce Couillet — along with input from experts in furnishings, foam, quilting, inflatable structures and printed cotton fabric — the resultant fan-shaped pillow expands, origami-like, with a simple touch of a switch. It can be used indoors or outside, on the ground, on a bed or a seat, allowing the user to adjust themselves, unaided.

Installed for the Sculpture by the Sea festival, artist Geraldo Zamproni wedged a stack of giant, inflatable pillows beneath a rock shelf along the Bondi to Coogee coastal walk, the sharp crags of the rock contrasting with the soft bulge of the cobalt blue pillows. Zamproni has previously presented his oversized installations in various locations across Europe, the USA and South America, squeezed in between the crevices of a building or trapped under concrete slabs. The interventions interrogate architecture and landscape, and provide a new perspective on space.

Project name: **Transformable Armchair Jacket**
Designer: **Moreno Ferrari for C.P. Company**
Location: **Italy** Date: **2001**

Created for Italian clothier C.P. Company, designer Moreno Ferrari's 'Transformable' line consists of PVC garments that morph into tents, inflatable armchairs and hammocks. This bright blue, waterproof, polyurethane jacket can be inflated with the in-built air compressor to become a low-slung, padded armchair. Another item, a poncho that could be redesigned as a tent, was displayed as part of an exhibition at the Centre Pompidou in Paris, France. The conceptual garments are the product of Ferrari's desire to create innovative and functional pieces that respond to the needs of city-dwellers.

Project name: **Skywhale**
Artist: **Patricia Piccinini**
Location: **Canberra, New South Wales, Australia** Date: **2013**

Artist Patricia Piccinini's enormous *Sky Whale* sculpture (an unearthly hot-air balloon of sorts) was rendered as a whale, but featured giant udders, rather than wings. Measuring 34 x 23 x 75 m (112 x 75 x 66 ft), the beast was created from 3,535 m (11,600 ft) of fabric sewn together with more than three million stitches. A commission to mark the centenary of the city of Canberra in New South Wales, Australia, Piccinini's work referenced the city's planned, artificial nature, and posits the question of what would have happened if evolution had taken a different turn.

Project name: **Sleeping Bag Dress**
Artist: **Ana Rewakowicz**
Location: **Mexico City, Mexico** Date: **2004**

Wearable as a kimono-style dress, this multipurpose garment converted into a sleeping
bubble that could fit up to two people. Inspired by the early pneumatic work of Archigram,
Ana Rewakowicz was concerned with the rise of materialism and waste. The dress provoked
a conversation about lightness; how to live and travel with less. Inflated by a fan powered
by batteries charged from a built-in solar panel, the wearer became self-sustainable in their
clothing-cum-portable shelter. It was road-tested in 2005 during her walking performances
in Mexico City, Mexico entitled *A Modern Day Nomad Who Moves As She Pleases*.

This site-specific intervention was installed in the cloister of a former convent as part of the CutOut Festa — a non-profit international animation and digital art festival — in Querétaro, Mexico. The massive cyan inflatable appropriated the entire space, embedding upon, and becoming part of, the architecture. It simultaneously gave the building a new identity, the plastic serving to dramatically highlight the detail of the late-seventeenth-century structure. Across the course of the day, sunlight permeated the translucent membrane from a glass dome above, meaning the constantly changing infusion of colour and light kept the monochrome work in a state of transformation.

Sasso Corbaro, a fourteenth-century castle located on the periphery of a small village in a rocky outcrop in the Swiss Alps, has been a UNESCO World Heritage Site since 2000. With this inflatable installation, artists Lang/Baumann created a dramatic intervention that established a paradoxical dialogue between old and new, solid and lightweight, permanent and ephemeral. The two silver-grey geometric forms are squares, encasing the monumental stonework. Measuring 5 x 5 m (16½ x 16½ ft), the bulky, bulging forms appear to sucker onto the stonework, both seeking refuge and providing sanctuary.

Despite its military-like appearance of a sandbag fortress, this igloo-shaped hideout is actually made of pillow-shaped inflatables, covered on the outside in brown vinyl and secured together with red strapping. The utilitarian exterior belies the cosy interior, which, in contrast, is clad in an assortment of colourful woollen blankets in banded layers. The shelter has a large opening in the top, not visible from outside, that allows light in. Installed inside the Design Museum in Helsinki, Finland, artist and designer Lambert Kamps' installation provided a play space for adults and children alike.

Situated in the seaside town of Pori, Finland, this installation consisted of a clear plastic geodesic dome that was inflated over the roof ventilator of a factory. A selection of potted plants were placed within the dome, investigating the capacity for plant life to absorb pollutants from the air; the air emitted from the vent was warm, creating a suitable environment for the plants, but it was also toxic. When NASA tested the air after a twenty-four hour period, it was confirmed that the plants were absorbing factory pollutants and adding a small amount of fresher air into the atmosphere.

Project name: **Inflatable Gallery**
Designer: **Melissa Berry**
Location: **Marfa, Texas, USA** Date: **2009**

Designed as a space for displaying artists' works at the El Cosmico festival in Texas, this prefabricated inflatable gallery was both lightweight and nomadic. Supported by a frame of PVC tubing, its body of three large plastic membranes was studded with a regular pattern of metal grommets. These gave a quilted effect and referenced the artists' hand-stitched works on display. Its attention-grabbing form was simply attached using plastic cable ties and duct tape — and easily erected within an afternoon. The billowing project gave shade from the unrelenting Texas sun during the day and created an undulating, illuminated frame by night.

Designed to celebrate the All Souls Day Festival in The Netherlands, this inflatable picnic pavilion centred on the wood-burning stove, which was used to prepare hot food and drinks as well as to heat the air that filled the pillowy canopy. Providing shelter for the picnickers below, the roof was held aloft by eight elongated timber trestles that were integrated into the pair of long tables and could seat up to forty people. At night, the roof was illuminated, acting as a beacon for the celebratory event and lighting the table and stove beneath.

This mirrored dome houses the spectacle of a simulated universe. Intended for inhabitants of big cities, where stargazing is a near-impossible activity due to air pollution, the silver hemisphere was first inflated beneath the A13 motorway in Canning Town, East London. Made from reflective silver Mylar — a material developed by NASA for space use in 1973 — laser beams bounced between layers of film, recreating the cosmos; designers Loop.pH used constellation maps to chart nearly 3,000 stars and planets. The immersive experience was complemented by an ambient soundscape.

Project name: **Occupancy**
Artist: **Hidemi Nishida**
Location: **Sapporo, Japan** Date: **2010**

This immersive installation by artist Hidemi Nishida involved a series of large-scale inflatable forms,
measuring approximately 18 x 8 m (59 x 26¼ ft). Sited in a school auditorium, the semi-darkened
room was almost entirely filled by the thirteen huge balloons of varying sizes — the largest over
4 m (13 ft) in diameter — made of agricultural plastic sheeting. Visitors could wend their way
through the interstitial spaces while colourful abstracted images were projected through the
transparent skins, creating a surreal, fluctuating spatial experience. The colour and light were
accompanied by a soundtrack, adding to the unearthly atmosphere.

Brazil-based Penique Productions' first intervention in the country was at the School of Visual Arts building of Parque Lage in Rio de Janeiro, at the foot of Corcovado mountain. For the site-specific project, they installed a huge orange inflatable within the building, highlighting its classical features. The balloon occupied the entire colonnaded courtyard space, protruding through the open rooftop of the structure (above). This allowed light to permeate the space, saturating the installation with an eerie glow. Part of a series, the work has travelled through countries including England, France, Italy, Portugal, Mexico and Lebanon.

The main stage for Norway's annual Kongsberg Jazz Festival, Snøhetta's membrane structure, Tuballoon, measures 20 m (65½ ft) in height and 40 m (130 ft) in length. A hybrid structure, it combines 1 m (3¼ ft) diameter inflatable perimeter tubes with an hourglass-shaped tension membrane, made from galvanized steel. Erected each year for the three-week festival, the structure is a dynamic and tuneable acoustic environment; its shapely form provides a classic clamshell-like shading over the audience to keep quiet performances intimate, while the PVC fabric construction is nearly transparent to sound during amplified performances.

This surreal space, an installation at a gallery in Rouyn-Noranda, Canada, is the interior of a golden-hued meteorological balloon, which was set within an enclosed, semi-airtight cube measuring 2½ m (8 ft) in each dimension. Usually the balloon rested deflated, the air removed by a blower. When a viewer approached artist Ana Rewakowicz's work, a motion detector triggered the blower that was sucking the air out. A negative pressure inside caused the balloon to inflate and fill the space, bulging at the portholes, and allowed a person to climb inside the opening to the sphere within.

Inflatable decoy planes and tanks were used in World War II as a creative deception tactic. The air-filled dummy tanks were made of rubber canvas and plywood, with drainpipes forming the gun.

Project name: **Mavericks**
Designer: **Heimplanet**
Location: **Hamburg, Germany** Date: **2014**

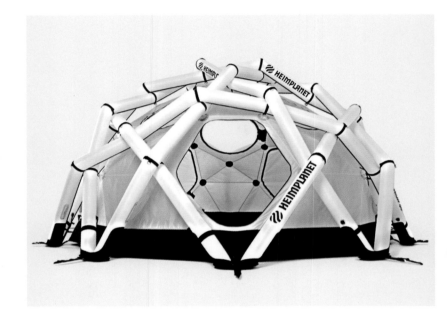

This tent was created to withstand extreme weather conditions, resisting wind speeds of up to 180 km (112 mi) per hour. Designed using geodesic principles, guy lines are only necessary in extreme conditions, and the airbeams can be inflated in a single step by one person and separated into multiple chambers if a part is damaged. With an internal height of 2 m (6½ ft) and more than 13 sq m (140 sq ft) of ground space, it can sleep up to ten people. The tent weighs 25 kg (55 lb) and has three doors, for easy access under all circumstances, and three windows. A series of closable vents at the bottom and the top offer ventilation.

Based on biological cell structure, Thomas Herzig's modular pneumatic building system offers an almost limitless number of possibilities for assembly. Made of one hundred per cent recyclable non-toxic TPU (thermoplastic polyurethane), modules of numerous shapes can be combined in multiple configurations to create stable constructions that are extremely lightweight, flame retardant and reusable; here, an inflated dome structure. On average, an inflated pneumocell construction has four hundred times less mass than a building made of brick and concrete of the same size, forty times less weight than a wooden building and half the weight of an ordinary tent.

Project name: **The Fantastic Trailer**
Designer: **Cheryl Baxter**
Location: **Bloomfield Hills, Michigan, USA** Date: **2012**

Suspended from a central lightweight structure, US designer Cheryl Baxter's colourfully illuminated canopies were made from 'draft' columns that used air in the same way as the attention grabbing 'air dancers' employed for advertising purposes. Each of the canopies comprised a modular, tri-column system, which created arcade-like spaces within. Air was pumped through the textile pieces and then slowly released through a small, metallic mesh strip in the centre seam, allowing the organza fabric to billow and the unconstrained 'legs' to move and dance in tune to the air movement.

Tapping into a desire for instant personal space in an often busy, crowded world, Anna Maria Cornelia created the Life Dress. The skirt section is zipped on before an air cartridge rapidly inflates it into a bubble that rises upwards, encasing the torso and head — it's advised that the wearer is sitting down for this bit. Ironically, while the dress allows the wearer to feel invisible to the outside world, its voluminous form and the bright yellow of the cocoon are quite an attention-grabbing sight.

Filling the cavernous atrium of the Guggenheim Museum in New York, this massive site-specific installation, created for a gala event, comprised 6,000 balloons. The sinuous form referenced the curves and swells of the architecture, while simultaneously juxtaposing the ephemerality of the balloons with the gravitas of the Guggenheim. Artist Jason Hackenwerth chose the inflatable medium for its accessibility; instead of contemporary art being daunting and unapproachable, the balloons were immediately identifiable as simplistic objects of joy and happiness. Following the event, *Aviary* was relocated to Catskill in upstate New York.

This 50 sq m (538 sq ft) pavilion, set up at the National School of Architecture in Paris, was an experimental prototype for an innovative construction system that combines an inflatable structure with an auxetic material. The structure became thicker in one or more width-wise directions when it was stretched along its length, conversely becoming thinner when compressed lengthwise. This was achieved through a folding pattern that created a tri-dimensional, form-changing surface. The result was an inflatable that could shrink, expand and multiply. The form created the opportunity for educational and playful interactions.

Project name: **Jello Pavilion**
Designer: **Cornell University**
Location: **Ithaca, New York, USA** Date: **2015**

Resembling a larger-than-life bird's egg, the Jello Pavilion was designed by students at Cornell University and inspired by the fun inflatable structures that came of age in the 1970s. Its spherical form is made from more than one hundred sheets of plastic sheeting, seared together to create a hermetic volume which is inflated by a high-power fan. Inside, balloons fill the space, providing a joyful retreat from end-of-semester stress. Costing less than three hundred dollars to construct, the Jello Pavilion is a fun reminder of the versatility of plastic.

Project name: **Loud Shadows**
Architect: **Plastique Fantastique**
Location: **Terschelling, The Netherlands** Date: **2017**

Loud Shadows was a three-part inflatable structure immersed within a forest setting on the island of Terschelling, The Netherlands, for the annual Oerol cultural festival. Two bubble domes — one transparent and one translucent — were connected by a doughnut-like tubular walkway, creating both internal and external environments to host live music and dance performances. The premise of the festival is to use the entire island as a stage, and the varied architecture of these pneumatic spaces created a dialogue with the surrounding woodland. The project was a collaboration between Kate Moore, The Soltz, LeineRoebana and Plastique Fantastique.

This bright, bulbous form, created by Spanish architects DOSIS, functioned as a playful and adaptable events space. The giant plastic enclosure is hard to miss with its distinctive transparent and yellow polka-dotted bubbles. The space is reconfigurable, able to transform from a single 65 sq m (700 sq ft) area into a multi-chamber structure of over 400 sq m (4,300 sq ft) in minutes. Its presence, pictured here in East London's London Fields, provided a curious, bold and fun insertion into public space.

This installation by Spanish architects PKMN was the winner of an architectural contest with a brief to bring contemporary art to places that lack an adequate exhibition infrastructure. Referencing the epic poem *Paradise Lost* by English poet John Milton, the work sought to insert an unfamiliar urban expression demarcated by its triangular metal framework. The orthogonal grid became the place under which Milton's Adam and Eve strolled, replacing the romantic notion of a walk below the treetops with a contemporary realization. The forest above was created not by foliage, but by a canopy of modular translucent inflatables.

Project name: **Pont de Singe**
Artist: **Olivier Grossetete**
Location: **Tatton Park, Cheshire, UK** Date: **2012**

French artist Olivier Grossetete used three giant helium-filled balloons to support his hazardous suspension bridge, which hovered with mystical appeal over a pond in Tatton Park, a historic estate in northwest England, as part of the Tatton Park Biennial. The *Pont de Singe*, which means Monkey Bridge, was theoretically capable of supporting the weight of a person, although its inaccessibility precluded this. The walkway was constructed from cedar wood, with its ends left to trail into the water. The bridge was a comment on the allure of opportunity and possibility — and its elusiveness — rendered in a picturesque form.

Like its namesake, this single-person shelter was dependent on a host: the outtake duct of another building's HVAC (heating, ventilation and air-conditioning) system. As warm air left the building, it entered the outer double-skin of the structure, simultaneously inflating and heating it. Artist Michael Rakowitz created the first *paraSITE* shelters from discarded materials; they cost approximately five dollars to make, and were given free of charge to the homeless in American cities on the east coast. *paraSITE* was a conspicuous social protest, not a long-term solution: 'These shelters should disappear like the problem should,' he said.

Ant Farm — an architecture, graphic arts and environmental design practice known for its counter-culture output throughout the 1970s — was established in San Francisco in 1968 by Chip Lord and Doug Michels and later joined by Curtis Schreier. Reacting to the monumentality of the Brutalist movement, Ant Farm proposed inflatable structures with no fixed form and beyond description in standard formats, questioning all the conventional tenets of architecture and construction. For this project, *Breathing — That's Your Bag*, visitors were invited to enter an enclosed pneumatic bubble to escape from the air pollution outside.

Developed by Polish design studio Zieta, these playful stools were created using an innovative forming process called FIDU (Freie Innen Druck Umformung), or Free Internal Pressure Forming. FIDU is the welding together of two ultra-thin steel sheets along their edges, which are then inflated under high pressure to produce a three-dimensional object. In addition to the Plopp stools, which come in various heights and colours, the range has expanded to include other lightweight, durable furniture and home accessories, such as mirrors, tables and wall decorations.

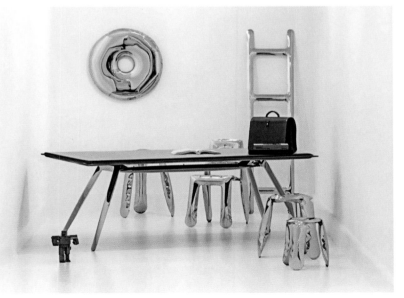

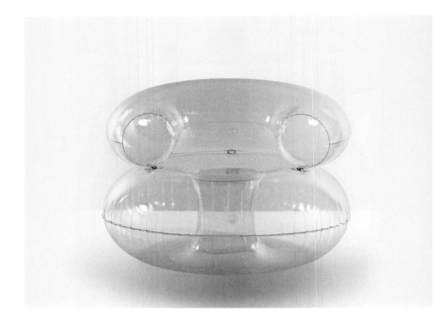

Vietnam-born, Paris-based designer Quasar Khanh launched his first inflatable furniture collection, called Aerospace, in 1968 (page 172). The Satellite No. 13 chair soon followed, produced by hand in a pool toy factory in the suburbs of Paris. Made from PVC, the chair consists of a simple circular base seat topped by a semi-circular arm-cum-backrest, connected by small metal rings. As with Khanh's other plastic pieces, the Satellite No. 13 chair was lightweight and inexpensive, with a lot of appeal to a pop-culture-ready audience. When it was launched it retailed for around six pounds, and was marketed as an 'exclamation point to the design of modern furniture!'

Project name: **CristalBubble**
Designer: **Pierre Stéphane Dumas**
Location: **France (or elsewhere)** Date: **2010**

One of a series of transparent, inflatable hotels, the CristalBubble is intended to replicate the pleasure of sleeping under the stars without sacrificing the comfort of shelter, bedding and other everyday luxuries. Easily dismounted and reassembled, the pods leave little to no impact on the space they inhabit, making the plastic igloo-like structures an unconventional solution for temporary accommodation. Completely transparent, they offer uninterrupted views of their natural surroundings. The CristalBubble is inflated by a noiseless ventilation system that filters air, prevents humidity and retains the spherical shape without framing or other structural support.

Comme des Garçons' Spring/Summer 2012 collection was entitled 'White Drama' and featured elaborate garments — flowered, frilled, layered and bowed — in all shades of white: pure, milky, chalky and ivory, from opaque to sheer. Each of the monochrome articles was intended to represent 'the great stages of life: birth, marriage, death and transcendence', according to designer Rei Kawakubo. Following the runway show, Kawakubo created a gallery exhibit that encased the collection in a series of transparent inflatable bubbles, transforming the work from fashion to art installation.

Artist Jason Hackenwerth was inspired by Greek mythology for this installation, which comprised 10,000 balloons intricately woven into a double-helix. *Pisces* was an interpretation of the myth of Aphrodite and Eros and their escape from the monster Typhon. In the story, they escaped Typhon by transforming into a woven spiral of two fish to avoid losing one another. This was later immortalized as the constellation Pisces: two fish twisting around each other. Suspended in the central atrium of the National Museum of Scotland in Edinburgh, it measured 12 m (40 ft) and was rendered in blue, greens and yellow.

'There's no angry way
to say "bubbles".'
Anon

Des Architectures Vives festival in Montpellier, France is an annual event held with the intention of creating an awareness of architecture for all. During this festival, many private courtyards are open to the public. These cloud-shaped seats were part of a series of surprise installation works in 2014 that highlighted often overlooked spaces. A cluster of silver inflated vinyl balls encased in a white translucent nylon mesh created lumpy, bubble-like forms that were both practical and whimsical. Easily movable and adaptable, they allowed visitors to sit or play in, on and around them.

Composer Arvo Pärt and Snøhetta collaborated on a series of 'Stillspots' around Lower Manhattan that explored the relationship between space and sound. Using sparse notes and low volumes in combination with his compositional style called *tintinnabuli* (Latin for little bells), Pärt, who describes his music as a 'frame for silence', created intimate soundscapes. In harmony with this, Snøhetta selected and altered five urban spaces — signified by large white inflatable orbs — that expanded the perception of sound in physical space. Pictured here is a green labyrinth created by the Battery Conservancy.

Part of the 10 Senses Festival in Valencia, Spain, this trio of inflatables was installed in locations around the Centre del Carme Cultura Contemporània (CCCC), an arts centre set within a former convent. Medusa, positioned in the gothic courtyard of the CCCC, provided a venue to host performing artists. The giant transparent doughnut formed an immersive arena where audience and stage became one; the mood was set by coloured illumination emanating from within. Bubble of the Senses encased an old well in the Renaissance courtyard, creating a meditative space, while The Vortex wormed along a colonnaded gallery space.

Unveiled as a pre-production prototype at the Salone del Mobile Milano in 1999, the Memo chair was a collaboration by architect and industrial designer Ron Arad and designer Nick Crosbie, the latter known for his inflatable pieces (page 128). Essentially a polystyrene-filled bag with a nozzle that allowed air to be added or removed, the piece changed from a soft bean bag to a hard seat in seconds. Inflated or deflated with a household vacuum cleaner or small pump, the Memo could also be sculpted into different shapes and floated well, making it a stable pool chair.

The Inflate range of products (page 128) was initially conceived in 1993; this whimsical egg cup, resembling a scaled-down inflatable pool ring, quickly became a design classic that is synonymous with the studio's output. Designer Nick Crosbie claims to 'like the hands-on immediacy ... I like to physically construct ... with inflatables, you can have an idea in the morning and have crafted the product by the end of the day.' Initially each item was handmade, but in due course they were mass produced to meet demand; the Egg Hoop eventually ceased production in 2000.

Project name: **Instant Untitled**
Architect: **MOS Architects**
Location: **Venice, Italy** Date: **2010**

Installed in the courtyard of the American pavilion at the Venice Biennale of Architecture 2010, this inflated canopy of oversized Mylar weather balloons was tethered to the ground with green ropes to create a simple yet striking entrance to the exhibition. Designed with Andy Warhol's 1966 *Silver Clouds* installation in mind, this commission was similarly arresting; its sparkling spheres glistening in the sun, mirroring the hue and shape of neighbouring tree foliage. The floating silvery surface provided relief from the Venetian sun for visitors, who could rest and meet on the white benches arranged in the courtyard below.

Project name: **Kiss the Frog**
Architect: **MMW Architects**
Location: **Oslo, Norway** Date: **2005**

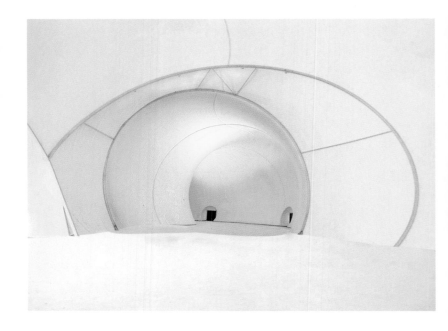

Kyss Frosken (meaning Kiss the Frog) was a vibrant green 2,000 sq m (21,527 sq ft) inflatable structure created as part of the celebrations for the 100th anniversary of Norway's independence from Sweden. Located on the future site of the new National Museum of Art, Architecture and Design, the frog symbolized the merger of four previously autonomous institutions: The National Gallery, the Museum of Architecture, the Museum of Contemporary Art and the Museum of Decorative Arts. The green membrane featured a fire retardant layer, while the inside had a white surface that allowed projections of digital media.

241

Project name: **Comfort #4**
Artist: **Lang/Baumann**
Location: **Môtiers, Switzerland** Date: **2011**

Entering into a wooden barn, situated in Môtiers, Switzerland, viewers were invited to participate in Lang/Baumann's installation, which formed part of the *Comfort* series, by climbing up one of two simple wooden ladders that disappeared through a void in the ceiling. The participant ascended towards the slot, emerging in the attic space to be confronted with a chaotic tangle of over 60 m (200 ft) of inflated white-PVC-coated fabric tubing. Measuring 95 cm (3 ft) in diameter, the bulging forms of the pipe-like structures twisted and overlapped, the beginning and ends of the tubes ambiguous, in striking contrast to the linear forms of the building.

Artist Shih Chieh Huang's work often engages with the low-tech, using inexpensive, off-the-shelf materials. Constructed from rolls of plastic drop sheets, more frequently used by painters, and blown up by simple household fans, the 120 m (400 ft) long worm-like form of this curious inflatable tumbled out across the courtyard of the Worcester Art Museum in Massachusetts, USA. Resembling intestines, or a giant sea creature, the lightweight material created an ephemeral installation that shifted and flailed as viewers interacted with it. This iteration was the largest in a series executed by Huang over a fifteen-year period.

Artist Ana Rewakowicz's *Uniblow Outfits* piece consisted of two inflatable suits, each constructed from a double layer of rubber latex with a cavity. The wearers donned the suits in their uninflated state, then walked around to activate the built-in foot pumps, which filled the cavity with air. With each step, the suits inflated further and, as they reached capacity, it became increasingly difficult for the wearers to continue moving. The suits were displayed in a shop front in Montréal, Canada; the work investigated issues surrounding strategies of fashion advertising and how they influence our understanding of the body.

As part of its fortieth anniversary celebrations, the Centre Pompidou in Paris staged an interactive exhibition that introduced children to four decades of art and design. Within the Galerie des Enfants, Studio GGSV created an installation in three parts, including playful sculptures, a performance by Chinese artist Liu Bolin, and this brightly coloured inflatable structure, Galeroom. Referencing works in the Centre Pompidou by artists such as René Magritte, Sol LeWitt, Karel Appel and Salvador Dalí, it sprang from the house's chimney to form a dome, which was illuminated by a marbled 'skylight'.

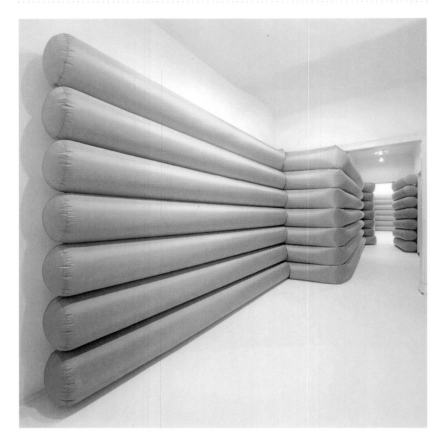

This site-specific installation at Galeria Foksal in Warsaw, Poland, was simultaneously determined, yet also distorted and transformed by, its context. Raising questions about the nature and perception of architectural space, seven large-scale, gold-hued inflatable polyester tubes sought to establish a dialogue with the surrounding built form, which had historically been a centre for the Polish avant-garde artists of the sixties. Reproducing the contours of the interior architecture, the seven stacked tubes, measuring 30 cm (12 in), altered the dimensions and acoustics of the gallery through their softly bulging layers.

Project name: **Sky Art Event**
Artist: **Otto Piene**
Location: **Berlin, Germany** Date: **2014**

German artist Otto Piene first began experimenting with what he called 'Sky Art' in 1967, using large-scale, spot-lit inflatables. For the closing ceremony of the ill-fated 1972 Summer Olympics in Munich, he created *Olympic Rainbow*, composed of five multi-coloured, helium-filled polythene tubes, each one 600 m (2,000 ft) long, which curved 125 m (410 ft) into the sky, forming an enormous arch that was visible over the stadium. A founder of the 1960s Düsseldorf-based Group Zero, Piene is also well known for his paintings made with smoke and fire.

Chrysalis was one of a series of interactive robotic artworks by Chico MacMurtrie that sought to provide a visceral experience of the minute geometric constructions that underlie all of life. The installation interacted with the audience on multiple levels, with its ever-changing geometries that responded upon a person's approach. Evocative of crystal-like formations, the work comprised one hundred interconnected tubes that were animated by compressed air via a servo-controlled computer system. When fully inflated, the tubes became a 12 m (40 ft) long, 8 m (26 ft) wide, 5 m (16 ft) high architectural, geometric space; when deflated, it returned to an organic form.

Project name: **Rebonds**
Artist: **Klaus Pinter**
Location: **Paris, France** Date: **2002**

Austrian artist Klaus Pinter was a founding member of the seminal Haus-Rucker-Co collective, which originated in Vienna in 1967. The group challenged conventions, creating new conceptual approaches and exploring the realm of pneumatic structures (page 181). Installed in the Panthéon in Paris, France, *Rebonds* was inspired by the work of Plato and his speculations on humanity and the physical world. The installation comprised two massive inflated spheres, one on the ground, the other poised on top, as if floating. The intricate detail of the building was reflected in, distorted and highlighted by the spheres.

Project name: **The Fabulous Inflated Villa**
Architect: **Luis Pons**
Location: **Miami Beach, Florida, USA** Date: **2005**

Miami-based architect Luis Pons created The Fabulous Inflated Villa as a commentary on his cityscape, which Pons said, 'failed to engage, and instead confronted an aggressively unattractive symbol of our architecturally inflated and environmentally impoverished age'. The pavilion critiqued the McMansion culture of the day, contending that the over-inflated real-estate market had caused Miamians to lose sight of detail and quality. Seven years later, in the wake of the world financial crisis, Pons reintroduced the work as an analogy for a different paradigm; the bubble had burst, so The Fabulous Inflated Villa was deflated (page 62).

Devised with the intention of reducing the use of fossil fuels, designer Alice Chun developed this inflatable and floatable solar lantern at the time of the Haiti earthquake in 2010. The possibilities for this remarkable invention are evident in areas struggling with poverty, refugee status and natural disasters. Weighing just 75 g (2½ oz) and measuring 11½ cm (4½ in) cubed, the SolarPuff is made of high-quality translucent, waterproof sailcloth. It packs flat then pops up into a soft, but durable cube that — from eight hours of bright sunlight — provides eight to twelve hours of portable lighting from ten powerful LEDs.

The Montgolfier brothers' first hot-air balloon flight in the 1780s launched a sheep, a duck and a rooster before King Louis XVI and 120,000 onlookers in France. They were airborne for fifteen minutes.

Project name: **Conversation Bubble**
Artist: **Ana Rewakowicz**
Location: **Ghent, New York, USA (or elsewhere)** Date: **2006**

This structure, made of clear vinyl, required the participation of five people in order to be inflated, each plugging a hole in the ellipsoid space. Cocooned within the base, the bodies of the participants were immobilized between layers of vinyl; their heads were unrestricted, but contained within the sphere, which became a literal speech bubble. The five people were free to chat for as long as the group agreed to continue, but the restrictions of this collaborative, interactive piece required a unanimous decision to keep going or end; no one person could leave of their own accord. The work was first exhibited at Art Omi gallery in Ghent, New York, USA.

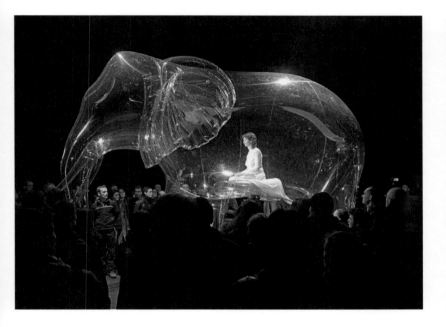

Swiss artist Victorine Müller's *Timeline* work took the form of a monolithic, transparent, inflatable elephant. Part-installation, part-performance art, part-sound work, the pneumatic piece was performed in Lucerne, Switzerland. Positioned within the belly of the beast, the artist sat cross-legged inside the form, which was lit from below, heightening a sense of intimacy. Later in the performance, the elephant was laid on its side, motionless and disempowered, as if sleeping or even dying. Müller described the PVC structure as: 'an elephant in a quiet, dark space, awe inspiring yet also arousing our sympathy.'

This interactive installation comprised one thousand 1¾ m (6 ft) high inflated plastic cylinders. Extending 200 m (656 ft) beneath a metro station bridge in Taipei, Taiwan, the work was a moment of surprise in a non-descript space. With vibrant hues at the base, the colours graduated to become transparent halfway up. The effect was reminiscent of an underwater coral garden — a seascape of anemones — creating a place of beauty and calm. The movement of people triggered LEDs causing them to twinkle, and some cylinders contained mini speakers that related stories of local history and interest.

The 'welcome' identifier and information point for Animac, an animated film festival held in Lleida, Spain, this flexible, transparent inflatable bubble was designed by Barcelona-based architects Vora. With a semi-transparent outer surface made of PVC and synthetic fibre, the structure could be used as a projection screen that was flexible enough to be positioned both indoors and out. Many of the interior fittings were recyclable: a sandbag bench running around the circumference was covered in waste fabric and also served to anchor the balloon to the ground.

This 24 m (79 ft) long, 12 m (39 ft) high balloon was installed outside the Parliament building as part of the celebrations for Stockholm's year as European Capital of Culture in 1998. The voluminous, egg-like form was flooded with artificial sunlight during the long hours of winter darkness. A later iteration was installed as part of the Light Festival in Helsingborg, Sweden, in which it was illuminated from within in a rotation of colours. In its final incarnation in 1999, the artist Monika Gora used it as the train of her own wedding dress.

Project name: **Untitled**
Architect: **Plastique Fantastique**
Location: **Madrid, Spain** Date: **2013**

These two giant egg-like inflatables were situated in a courtyard at IED Madrid, the Spanish capital's largest design school. The twin inflatables were the result of a workshop led by Marco Canevacci, founder of collective Plastique Fantastique, in which Canevacci and students of IED sought to investigate concepts of public and private and the use, habitability and function of urban space. The concept of synaesthesia was proposed by the students as the inspiration for the output of the week-long event, culminating in the creation of these transparent structures.

The National Space Centre, located on a riverbank in the city of Leicester, England, UK occupies the footprint of a disused stormwater tank. Combining an exhibition centre with a research and education facility, the building is dominated by the 40 m (131 ft) high transparent tower, which contains two large rockets. The skin of the tower is constructed of inflated ETFE (ethylene tetrafluoroethylene) panels over a lightweight steel frame. The translucent cladding has varying opacity levels, depending on time of day and angle of view, which permit visibility of the rockets from outside, and views of Leicester from the decks within.

Project name: **Towered**
Artist: **Steve Messam**
Location: **Gordon, Scotland, UK** Date: **2017**

Like *Pointed* (page 26), *Towered* was created as part of a trio of works, called *XXX*, that were situated within the grounds of eighteenth-century Mellerstain House in Gordan, Scotland, UK. The environmental artist Steve Messam sought to establish a playful dialogue between the old and the new, permanent and ephemeral, and *Towered* was a surprising and delightful intervention within a picturesque sculpture park. Stark white inflatable tubes rose over 8 m (26 ft) from within the ruins of an old stone building that, hundreds of years ago, had been a laundry outhouse. Extending the architectural space of the relic, Messam also played with perception of scale.

Exploring themes of power and governance, as well as of deferred gratification, artist Tom Dale created a 6 m (20 ft) tall inflated castle that mimicked the architectural grandiosity often associated with institutions of bureaucracy. The crenelated black vinyl bouncy house, exhibited at Copperfield gallery in London, England, UK, was intended to draw viewers in with a child-like desire to interact. However, they were forbidden to enter the work, the intention being to play on the frustration often experienced at the hands of government, and so highlight the seeming exclusivity of the 'towers of power'.

Project name: **Wall to Wall, Floor to Ceiling**
Artist: **Alex Schweder**
Location: **Tel Aviv, Israel** Date: **2014**

Commissioned by the Tel Aviv Museum of Art, Israel, this work featured twelve large inflatables — six attached to the ceiling in white, and six on the floor in grey — which appeared to breathe asynchronously from both above and below. As they continuously pushed one another out of the way, the space was reconfigured. Sections of the inflatables were furry, enticing people to interact with the protrusions, suggestive of doors, seats and beds, which were constantly in a state of flux. An audio work by Andy Graydon delivered pseudo gallery attendant behavioural warnings.

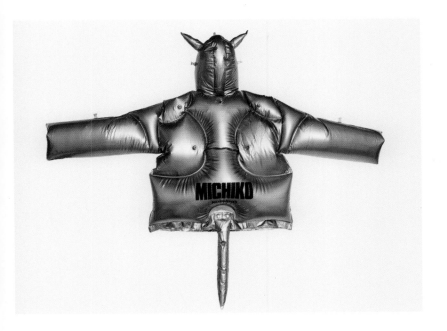

Japanese-born English designer Michiko Koshino launched her fashion brand in 1981 with a shop in London's Covent Garden. Rising to fame in the early 1990s with the support of club kids and celebrities such as David Bowie and Stella McCartney, Koshino's much-copied inflatable coats are instantly recognisable. Of the collection, this is perhaps the most iconic; a silver PVC inflatable jacket that can be worn inflated or deflated, adjustable through nineteen individual air pumps. The cult garment also features a hood with cat ears, with a detachable tail adding a characteristic whimsical detail.

Using colourful, sausage-shaped party balloons, designer Seung Jin Yang had the intention to '... turn a simple making process based on personal childhood memories into an industrial fabrication furniture-making process'. His resulting collection features chairs and stools made by applying eight layers of clear epoxy resin over the modelled balloons. Each layer takes half a day to complete, with successive resin layers gradually added on top. Thus, the process of creating a single stool takes around one week. Despite their fragile appearance, the seats have a glossy, rigid outer surface that is able to support the weight of a person.

An initiative of the Rotterdam Climate Proof programme, this floating pavilion is a pioneering example of innovative and sustainable architecture. The pavilion comprises three connected hemispheres currently used for exhibitions and events, but it is in fact a prototype for a floating home. Anchored within Rotterdam's old harbour, the structure is constructed to adapt to rising sea-levels. With a translucent shell of ETFE (ethylene tetrafluoroethylene), a super-strong, anti-corrosive plastic one hundred times lighter than glass, the air-filled panels are an ideal floating material.

This self-supporting structure was first displayed at DMY Berlin, an annual contemporary design festival. Designer and artist Lambert Kamps, based in Groningen, The Netherlands, created this inflatable edifice to host both indoor and outdoor events. The pavilion was constructed from more than 130 connected pillows of air that formed a tunnel-like space and provided an intimate enclosure, with varying sizes of airbags being used to give the structure its shape. The Pillow Tent could be customized and reinstalled for temporary events, such as festivals and exhibitions.

Project name: **NAWA**
Designer: **Zieta Prozessdesign Studio**
Location: **Wrocław, Poland** Date: **2017**

Erected on Daliowa Island in the Odra river in Wrocław, Poland, this graceful pavilion of thirty-five highly polished, connected steel arches was commissioned as part of a restoration project of the space following floods in the 1990s. Forming a sleek gateway onto the island, the sculpture was created using FIDU technology (Freie Innen Druck Umformung), or Free Internal Pressure Forming, a process which Polish design studio Zieta has used to make smaller objects such as stools (page 224). The metal forms are durable and stable, but also light; NAWA was Zieta's first FIDU construction on a large scale.

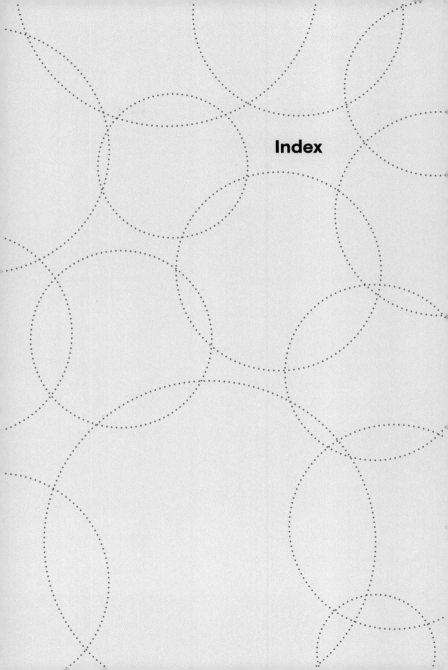

Index

Directory of Architects, Artists and Designers

Agis, Maurice
135

Airclad
82, 189

Alfaya, Luciano G
188

amid.cero9
126

Ant Farm
182, 223

Arad, Ron
236

Architects of Air
66

Atelier Zündel Criste
30

Azua, Martin
144

Backer, Pascale de
107

Balenciaga
116

Banchini, Leopold
41

Barotti, Marco
111, 132

Baxter, Cheryl
212

Bellini, Mario
54

Berrux, Fabrice
77

Berry, Melissa
200

Bina Baitel Studio
190

Bjarke Ingels Group (BIG)
46

Blofield
52, 124

Borland, Ralph
136

Buck, Kim
16, 120

Buildair
167

Byrne, David
168

Chalayan, Hussein
96

Chas, Cipriano
188

Christo
134

Chromat
72

Chun, Alice
251

City Yeast
256

Cloud 9
29, 36

Comme des Garçons
228

Cornelia, Anna Maria
213

Cornell University
216

Couillet, Luce
190

Dale, Tom
263

Deller, Jeremy
45

Deltasync
268

Design Office Takebayashi Scroggin (D.O.T.S.)
232

DOSIS
218

Dumas, Pierre Stéphane
227

Dynamorphe
215

Estudio 3.14
31

Ferrari, Moreno
11, 192

Flavel, Norton
113

Förster, Monica
57

Friends with You
79, 105

Google
169

Gora, Monika
259

Grimshaw Architects
106

National Space Centre
261

Grossetete, Olivier
221

Guy, Tehila
98

Hackenwerth, Jason
214, 229

Hale, Mary
170

Heimplanet
43, 210

Hemmert, Hans
176

Herzig, Thomas
211

Herzog & de Meuron
146

Hidemi Nishida Studio
49

Hövding
56

Huang, Shih Chieh
243

Imaisde Design Studio
104

Inflate
48, 117, 128, 140, 166,
189, 236, 237

Isozaki, Arata
88

Issey Miyake
178

Jiakun Architects
108

Kamps, Lambert
73, 147, 150, 198, 269

Kapoor, Anish
88, 148

Kauste, Juulia
75

Kengo Kuma & Associates
141

Khanh, Quasar
172, 226

Klymit
72

Koshino, Michiko
265

Kuehnle, Jimmy
152, 171

Kulve, Thor ter
99

Kusama, Yayoi
153

Lang/Baumann
197, 242, 246

LIKEArchitects
78

Locke, John
119

Loop.pH
202

Lundén, Eero
75

McCharen-Tran, Becca
72

McKay, Alan
80

MacMurtrie, Chico
248

MAD Architects
97

Malafor
92

Martin, Mickaël
155

Mass Studios
175

Maurer, Ingo
86

Melnyk, Virginia
68

Meritalian
54

Messam, Steve
24, 262

Meumann, Kiri-Una Brito
22

Miyake, issey
178

MMW Architects
240

Möller, Theo
86

Moon Ji Bang
32

MOS Architects
238

Mossine Partners
159

MPOWERD
161

Müller, Hans-Walter
19

Müller, Victorine
83, 139, 255

Muñiz, Patricia
188

Murphy, Clive
125

Nishida, Hidemi
204

Numen/For Use
50, 184

Ohana, Eden
58

OMA
90, 179

Overtreders W
201

Panton, Verner
90

Penique Productions
115, 127, 138, 196, 205

Penttinen Schöne
100, 140

Petillon, Charles
23

Piccinini, Patricia
193

Piene, Otto
247

Pinter, Klaus
181, 249

PKMN Architects
220

Plastique Fantastique
35, 53, 71, 74, 88, 111, 132,
160, 180, 217, 234, 260

Pneuhaus
37, 69, 174

Pons, Luis
62, 250

Pot, Bertjan
118, 158

PTW Architects
26

Public Domain Architects
268

Pugh, Gareth
51

Raeburn, Christopher
40

Rakowitz, Michael
222

Randall-Page, Thomas
182

Raumlabor
110, 112

Reinoso, Pablo
93

Rewakowicz, Ana
20, 194, 199, 207, 244, 254

Reyes, Joaquin
119

Roche Bobois
77

Rodot, Margaux
155

Rogers, Benedetta
182

Santachiara, Denis
28

Schweder, Alex
21, 63, 137, 264

Seattle Design Nerds
18

SelgasCano
131

Seung Jin Yang
266

Slow Studio
25

Smigla-Bobinski, Karina
85

Snarkitecture
154

Snøhetta
206, 233

Spatial Effects
162

Starck, Phillipe
185

Studio GGSV
245

Studio MMASA
188

Takizawa, Naoki
178

Tastet, Benoît
155

teamLab
94

Toer
151

Topotek 1
70

Traft
157

Vancil, Darren
156

Vives, Carolina González
177

Vogler, Andreas
42

Vora Arquitectura
258

Walala, Camille
76

Wanders, Marcel
65

Yael Reisner Studio
114

Yamamoto, Yohji
64

Zamarbide, Daniel
41

Zamproni, Geraldo
84, 191

Zanotta
77, 130

Zieta Prozessdesign Studio
44, 224, 270

Index

Page numbers in *italics* refer
to illustrations

10 Senses Festival 234
48 Hours Neukölln 180, *180*

A

ADA 85, *85*
AeroMorph *12–13*
Agis, Maurice 135, *135*
Air Bridge 147, *147*
Air Cleanser 199, *199*
Air Flower 77, *77*
Air Forest 175, *175*
Air Lounger 48, *48*
Airbag Helmet 56, *56*
Airclad
   Badboot Boat 82, *82*
   Snoozy 189, *189*
AirDraft 182, *182–3*
airships 7–8
Alfaya, Luciano G 188, *188*
All Souls Day Festival 201
Allianz Arena 146, *146*
Almost Nothing 125, *125*
American Institute of
Architects 170
amid.cero9 126, *126*
AMO 90
Anda 98, *98*
Andalucía Museum of
   Memory 84
Anderegg, Anna 111
Anderson, Orvil 8
The Animac Bubble 258, *258*
Another Generosity 75, *75*
Ant Farm 9, 10, 182
   Clean Air Pod 223, *223*
Aphrodite 229
Apollo Chair 172, *172*
Appel, Karel 245
Arad, Ron 236, *236*
Archigram 9, 10, 11, 194
Architects of Air 66, *66*, 67
architecture 9, 11, 12
ArchTriumph 30
Ark Nova 88, *88*

Arlandes, Marquis François
   Laurent d' 7
Art Basel, Miami 105
Art en Plein, Môtier 139
art installations 10
Art Omi, Ghent, New York 254
Art Production Fund 79
Au premier matin 181, *181*
Aviary 214, *214*
Azua, Martin 144, *144*, *145*

B

Bachelard, Gaston 41
Backer, Pascale de 107, *107*
Bacon, Francis 15
Badboot Boat 82, *82*
Baitel, Bina 190, *190*
Balenciaga 116, *116*
Balloon Cluster Lamps 118, *118*
Balloon Saloon 122
balloons 12
   hot-air balloons 7, 8, 252
Balmond, Cecil 179
Banchini, Leopold 41, *41*
Barotti, Marco 111, *111*, 132,
   132, *133*
Basic Home 144, *144*, *145*
Battery Conservancy,
   New York City 233
Baxter, Cheryl 212, *212*
Baywatch 164
BCN re.set pavilion series 114
Beach Cocoon 107, *107*
Beijing Design Week 97
Beijing National Aquatics
   Centre 26, *26–7*
Beijing Summer Olympics
   (2008) 11, 26, *26–7*
Bellini, Mario 54, *54–5*
Beirut Art Fair 127
A Better World By Design
   conference 174
Berrux, Fabrice 77, *77*
Berry, Melissa 200, *200*
Beyoncé 51
Big Air Package 134, *134*
Big Blo 2-Seater 124, *124*
Bina Baitel Studio 190, *190*
bioregenerative life support
   systems 13

Bird, Walter 9
Birdair Structures Inc. 9
Bjarke Ingels Group (BIG)
   46, *46–7*
Blofield
   Big Blo 2-Seater 124, *124*
   DoNut 52, *52*
Bloostar 12
Blow Chair 77, 130, *130*
Blow Me Up 86, *86*, *87*
Blow Sofa 92, *92*
Blowing Balloon Collection
   266, *266*, *267*
Blowing Molds 58, *58*, *59*
Borland, Ralph 136, *136*
Bowie, David 265
Branson, Richard 8
Brown University 174
Brutalism 9, 223
BuBble 188, *188*
Bubble Dome 37, *37*
Bublik 156
Buck, Kim
   Dobbeltriflet Opblæst
   spoons 16, *16*
   Opblæst Ring 120, *120*
   Puffed Up Pendants 120, *121*
   Puffed Up Vase 16, 17
Buildair 167, *167*
Bulk Carrier 113, *113*
Bund Schweizer Architekten 41
Byrne, David 168, *168*

C

C. P. Company 192
Calatrava, Santiago 35
camera obscura 69
Ca.mia 30, *30*
Canevacci, Marco 260
Carbon Balloon Chair 65, *65*
Carroll, Lewis 97
Cassidy, John 122
Caterpillar Tent 73, *73*
Centre del Carme Cultura
   Contemporània (CCCC),
   Valencia 234
Centre Pompidou, Paris
   192, 245
Centre for Visual Arts,
   Groningen 150

Chalayan, Hussein 51, 96, *96*
Chas, Cipriano 188, *188*
Chat Inflatables 104, *104*
C!here Art Crawl 68
Chesterfield Sofa 172, 173
Christo 10, 134, *134*
Chromat 72, *72*
Chrysalis 248, *248*
Chun, Alice 12, 251, *251*
City Yeast 256, *256*, *257*
Clean Air Pod 223, *223*
The Cloud 185, *185*
Cloud 9
  Media-ICT Building 29, *29*
  Thirst Pavilion 36, *36*
Cloud Berlin 74, *74*
Cloud Garden 232, *232*
Cloud Observatory 177, *177*
Cloud Room Divider 57, *57*
Colomina, Beatriz 41
Comfort #4 242, *242*
Comfort #8 246, *246*
Comfort #13 197, *197*
Comme des Garçons
  228, *228*
communications 12
Compound Camera 69, *69*
Concéntrico 180
Conversation Bubble
  254, *254*
Coop Himmelb(lau) 9
Copperfield gallery,
  London 263
Cornelia, Anna Maria 11,
  213, *213*
Cornell Aeronautical
  Lab 9
Cornell University 216, *216*
Cosy Shelter 198, *198*
Cosy Structure 191, *191*
Couillet, Luce 190, *190*
Covent Garden Market
  Building 23, *23*
Creature Craft 156, *156*
CristalBubble 227, *227*
Crosbie, Nick 117, 128
  Egg Hoop 237, *237*
  Memo Chair 236, *236*
Cumulus Parasol 151, *151*
CutOut Festa, Querétaro
  196

D

Dactiloscopia Rosa 71, *71*
Dale, Tom 263, *263*
Dalí, Salvador 245
Dazed 51
deCordova Sculpture Park
  and Museum, Lincoln,
  Massachusetts 137
Deflated Villa 62, *62*
Deller, Jeremy 45, *45*
Deltasync 268, *268*
Department of the Interior
  263
Des Architectures Vives 232
Descartes, René 7
DesertSeal 42, *42*
Design Museum, Helsinki 198
DesignMiami/ 154
Design Office Takebayashi
  Scroggin (D.O.T.S.)
  232, *232*
Diller Scofidio + Renfro 11
Diodon Project 215, *215*
Un dixième Printemps
  155, *155*
DMY Berlin 269
Dobbeltriflet Opblæst
  spoons 16, *16*
DoNut 52, *52*
DOSIS 218, *218*, *219*
Dreamspace 135, *135*
Drift 154, *154*
A Drop of Light 259, *259*
Dumas, Pierre Stéphane
  227, *227*
Dynamorphe 12, 215, *215*

E

Eden Project 106, *106*
Egg Hoop 237, *237*
El Claustro 196, *196*
English National Ballet 110
The Enlightenment 7
Erdling 83, *83*
Eros 229
Espaco 180 138, *138*
Essex County Council 140
Estar Azul 115, *115*
Estudio 3.14 31, *31*

ETFE (ethylene
  tetrafluoroethylene) 11
European Capital of Culture
  (1998), Stockholm 259
Ewen, Hunter 38
Explorer II 8

F

*The Fabulous Inflated
  Villa* 250, *250*
The Fantastic Trailer 212, *212*
fashion 11
Federation of Swiss Architects
  (FSA) 41
Ferrari, Moreno 11, 192, *192*
Festival Arbres en Lumières
  139
Festival IN 138
Fiberthin Air Houses 9
FIDU (Freie Innen Druck
  Umformung) technology
  44, 224, 270
FIFA World Cup (2006) 11
Flavel, Norton 113, *113*
Floating Pavilion 268, *268*
Fondation d'Entreprise
  Martell 131
Förster, Monica 57, *57*
Le fort de Schoenenbourg 83
Fossett, Steve 8
Foster and Partners Architects
  13
Fragile Occupancy Cloud
  49, *49*
Friends with You
  Light Cave 79, *79*
  Rainbow City 105, *105*
furniture 11
FYF Fest 49

G

Galeria Foksal, Warsaw 246
Galeroom 245, *245*
Galicia Contemporary Arts
  Centre 176
Gasometer Oberhausen,
  Germany 134
Gelbes Herz (Yellow Heart) 10

Ghost Army 8–9
Glasgow International Festival of Visual Art 45
The Golden Balloon 126, *126*
Google 12, 169, *169*
Gora, Monika 259, *259*
Grand Palais, Paris 148
Graydon, Andy 264
Grenada Millennium Biennale (2012) 84
Grimshaw Architects
 Eden Project 11, 106, *106*
 National Space Centre 261
Grinda, Efrén García 126
Grossetete, Olivier 221, *221*
Group Zero 247
Guggenheim Museum, New York 214
Guidepost to the Eternal Space 153, 153
Guy, Tehila 11, 98, *98*
Gvasalia, Demna 116

H

Hanami 155
Hackenwerth, Jason
 Aviary 214, *214*
 Pisces 229, *229*
Hale, Mary 170, *170*
Hanger H54 167, *167*
Haus-Rucker-Co 9, 10, 249
Heartbeat 23, *23*
Heimplanet
 Mavericks 210, *210*
 The Wedge 43, *43*
Hemmert, Hans 176, *176*
Herzig, Thomas 211, *211*
Herzog & de Meuron 11, 146, *146*
Hidemi Nishida Studio 49, *49*
High Altitude Airship (HAA) 12
High Line, New York 105, 168
Hincks, Anthony T 143
Hindenburg disaster 8

Hollowware bowl 16, *17*
Homogenizing and Transforming World 94, *94*, 95
hot-air balloons 7, 8, 252
housing 9, 12
Hövding 56, *56*
Huang, Shih Chieh 243, *243*
Hussein Chalayan's Spring 2017 Ready-to-Wear 96, *96*
Hyde Park, London 179

I

IED Madrid 260
Imaisde Design Studio 104, *104*
Inflate
 Air Lounger 48, *48*
 Chair 117, *117*
 Egg Hoop 237, *237*
 Inflatable Space 140, *140*
 Memo Chair 236, *236*
 Office in a Bucket 166, *166*
 Snoozy 189, *189*
 Wine Rack and Star Vase 128, *128*, *129*
Inflatable Cat Jacket 265, *265*
Inflatable Dress 72, *72*
Inflatable Gallery 200, *200*
Inflatable RGBubble 174, *174*
Inflatable Space 140, *140*
Inflatable Striped Nylon Dress 51, *51*
Inflato Dumpster 119, *119*
Inside Out 20, *20*
Instant Untitled 238, *238–9*
Institute for Advanced Architecture 13
International Expo, Zaragoza (2008) 36
Internet 12
Isozaki, Arata 12, 88, *88*
Issey Miyake 178, *178*
Itinerant Home 170, *170*

J

Jello Pavilion 216, *216*

K

Kamps, Lambert
 Airbridge 147, *147*
 Caterpillar Tent 73, *73*
 Cosy Shelter 198, *198*
 Pillow Tent 269, *269*
 Video Folly 150, *150*
Kapoor, Anish
 Ark Nova 12, 88, *88*
 Leviathan 148, *148*, *149*
Kauste, Juulia 75, *75*
Kawakubo, Rei 228
Kengo Kuma & Associates 141, *141*
Kiss The Frog 240, *240*, *241*
Khanh, Quasar
 Apollo Chair 11, 172, *172*, *173*
 Satellite No. 13 Chair 226, *226*
Klymit 72, *72*
Kongsberg Jazz Festival 206
Koolhaas, Rem 179, *179*
Koshino, Michiko 265, *265*
Kuehnle, Jimmy
 Stuffed Full 152, *152*
 You Wear What I Wear 171, *171*
Kulve, Thor Ter 99, *99*
Kusama, Yayoi 153, *153*

L

Labyrinth 111, *111*
Lady Gaga 51
Lang/Baumann
 Comfort #4 242, *242*
 Comfort #8 246, *246*
 Comfort #13 197, *197*
Leech, Adam 89
LeineRoebana 217
Leviathan 148, *148*, *149*
LeWitt, Sol 245
Life Dress 213, *213*
Light Cave 79, *79*
Light Festival, Helsingborg 259
lighting 12
LIKEArchitects 78, *78*
Lindstrand, Per 8
Liu Bolin 245

Lively Architecture Festival, Montpellier 155
Living in a Bubble 207, *207*
Locke, John 119, *119*
Lockheed Martin 12
Lohia, Ramesh and Surbhi 61
London Design Festival 76
London Festival for Architecture 110
Loop.pH 10, 202, *202*, *203*
Lord, Chip 223
Loud Shadows 217, *217*
Louis XVI, King 252
Luci 161, *161*
Luftschiff Zeppelin 1 (LZ1) 7–8
Luminaria 66, *66*, *67*
Lundén, Eero 75, *75*

M

McCartney, Stella 51, 265
McCharen-Tran, Becca 72, *72*
McKay, Alan 80
Mack Sennett Studios 49
McKay, Alan 80
MacMurtrie, Chico 12, 248, *248*
MAD Architects 97, *97*
Magritte, René 245
Malafor 92, *92*
Mars 13, 42
Martin, Mickaël 155, *155*
Mass Studios 175, *175*
Matadero Madrid 71
Maurer, Ingo 86, *86*, *87*
Mavericks 210, *210*
Media-ICT Building 29, *29*
Mellerstain House, Gordan, Scotland 24, *24*, 262
Memo Chair 236, *236*
Melnyk, Virginia 68, *68*
Meritalian 54, *54–5*
Messam, Steve
    Pointed 24, *24*
    Towered 262, *262*
Meumann, Kiri-Una Brito 11, 22, *22*
Meusnier, Jean Baptiste 7
Michels, Doug 223

Microcity Sales Office 159, *159*
Miller, William H 158
Milne, AA 187
Milton, John 220
miniGAGARIN 35, *35*
MIT Media Lab 12–13
Miyake, Issey 178, *178*
MMW Architects 240, *240*, *241*
Moderna Museet Malmö 89, *89*
Möller, Theo 86, *86*, *87*
Le Moment Végétatif 139, *139*
Momo at the Souks 127, *127*
Montfolfier brothers 7, 252
Moon Ji Bang 32, *32*, *33*
Moore, Kate 217
Moreno, Cristina Díaz 126
MOS Architects 238, *238–9*
Mossine Partners 159, *159*
MPOWERD 12, 161, *161*
Müller, Hans-Walter 19, *19*
Müller, Victorine
    Erdling 83, *83*
    Le Moment Végétatif 139, *139*
    Timeline 255, *255*
Munich Summer Olympics (1972) 247
Muñiz, Patricia 188, *188*
Murakami, Haruki 103
Murphy, Clive 125, 125
Murphy, Róisin 51
Musée des Arts Décoratifs (MAD), Paris 172
Museum of Applied Art, Frankfurt 141
Museum of Architecture, Oslo 240
Museum of Arts and Sciences, Valencia 35
Museum of Contemporary Art, Oslo 240
Museum of Contemporary Art, Tokyo 126
Museum of Decorative Arts, Oslo 240
Museum of Modern Art, New York 32, 130
Mylar 202

N

NASA 13, 199, 202
The National Gallery, Oslo 240
National Museum of Art, Architecture and Design, Oslo 240
National Museum of Modern and Contemporary Art, Seoul 32
National Museum of Scotland, Edinburgh 229
National School of Architecture, Paris 215
National Space Centre, Leicester 261, *261*
The Nature of Motion 158, *158*
NAWA 270, *270–1*
Net Blow-Up 50, *50*
New Collection, Munich 130
Nishida, Hidemi 204, *204*
Numen/For Use
    Net Blow-Up 50, *50*
    String Vienna 184, *184*
Nylund, Felix 53

O

O Mundo ao Contrário 78
Oase No. 7 10
Occupancy 204, *204*
Oerol Festival 217
Ohana, Eden 58, *58*, *59*
Olympic Games
    Beijing (2008) 11, 26, *26–7*
    Munich (1972) 247
OMA
    Prada Spring/Summer 2019 Menswear 90, *90–1*
    Serpentine Pavilion 179, *179*
onduline 131
Orblaest Ring 120, *120*
Organic Concept 243, *243*
Osmo 202, *202*, *203*
Overtreders W 201, *201*

P

Pace Gallery 168
Panton, Verner 90, *90–1*

Panthéon, Paris 249
Paradise Lost 220, *220*
paraSITE shelters 222, *222*
Parkbench Bubble 99, *99*
Parkinson, Alan 66
La Parole 93, *93*
Pärt, Arvo 233
Pawtuckets Art Festival 69
Peace 25, *25*
Peace Pavilion 30, *30*
Penique Productions
  El Claustro 10, 196, *196*
  Espaco 180 138, *138*
  Estar Azul 115, *115*
  Momo at the Souks
  127, *127*
  A Piscina do Parque
  Lage 205, *205*
Penttinen, Emma 140
Penttinen Schöne 140, *140*
  RedBall Project 10, 100,
  100, *101*
The People Speak 140
Petillon, Charles 23, *23*
Piccard, Auguste 8
Piccinini, Patricia 193, *193*
Piene, Otto 247, *247*
Pilâtre de Rozier, Jean-
  François 7
Pillow Tent 269, *269*
Pinter, Klaus
  Au premier matin 181, *181*
  Rebonds 249, *249*
Pisces 229
A Piscina do Parque Lage
  205, *205*
PKMN Architects 220, *220*
Plastique Fantastique
  Cloud Berlin 74, *74*
  Dactiloscopia Rosa 71, *71*
  Labyrinth 111, *111*
  Loud Shadows 217, *217*
  miniGAGARIN 35, *35*
  Moderna Museet Malmö
  89, *89*
  Pneumapolis 234, *234*,
  235
  RINGdeLUXE 180, *180*
  SiloSilo 160, *160*
  Sound of Light 10, 132,
  132, *133*

superKOLMEMEN 53, *53*
  Untitled 260, *260*
Plato 249
playLAND 78, *78*
Plopp Stool 224, *224*, *225*
Pneuhaus
  Bubble Dome 37, *37*
  Compound Camera 69, *69*
  Inflatable RGBubble 174, *174*
Pneumapolis 234, *234*, *235*
Pneumocell 211, *211*
Pointed 24, *24*
Pons, Luis
  Deflated Villa 62, *62*
  The Fabulous Inflated Villa
  250, *250*
Pont de Singe 221, *221*
'pop' design movement 130
Portavilion 110, *110*
Pot, Bertjan
  Balloon Cluster Lamps
  118, *118*
  The Nature of Motion
  158, *158*
Prada Spring/Summer 2019
  Menswear 90, *90–1*
Project Loom 169, *169*
PTW Architects 26, *26–7*
Public Domain Architects
  268, *268*
Puffed Up Pendants 120, *121*
Puffed Up Vase 16
Pugh, Gareth 51, *51*

R

Raeburn, Christopher 40, *40*
radomes 9
Rainbow City 105, *105*
Rakowitz, Michael 12, 222,
  222
Randall-Page, Thomas 182,
  182–3
Raumlabor
  Portavilion 110, *110*
  Spacebuster 112, *112*
Rebonds 249, *249*
RedBall Project 100,
  100, *101*
ReFractor 18, *18*
Regent's Canal 182

Reinoso, Pablo 93, *93*
Rendez-vous avec la Vi(ll)e
  19, *19*
Restless Sphere 9
Rewakowicz, Ana
  Air Cleanser 199, *199*
  Conversation Bubble
  254, *254*
  Inside Out 20, *20*
  Living in a Bubble 207, *207*
  Sleeping Bag Dress 11, 194,
  194, *195*
  Uniblow Outfits 244, *244*
Reyes, Joaquin 119, *119*
RINGdeLUXE 180, *180*
Roche Bobois 77, *77*
Rodot, Margaux 155, *155*
Rogers, Benedetta 182, *182–3*
The Roof That Goes Up in
  Smoke 201, *201*
Roomograph 137, *137*
Rotterdam Climate Proof
  programme 268

S

A Sac of Rooms All Day Long
  63, *63*
Sacrilege 45, *45*
Salone del Mobile Milano 236
SaloneSatellite (2017) 107
San Francisco Museum of
  Modern Art (SFMOMA)
  23, 63
Santachiara, Denis 28, *28*
São Paulo Design Weekend
  115
Sasso Corbaro 197
Satellite No. 13 Chair 226, *226*
satellites 12
Schöne, Philip 140
School of Visual Arts, Rio de
  Janeiro 205
Schreier, Curtis 223
Schweder, Alex
  Roomograph 137, *137*
  *A Sac of Rooms All Day
  Long* 63, *63*
  Snowballing Doorway 21, *21*
  *Wall to Wall, Floor to
  Ceiling* 10, 264, *264*

Sculpture by the Sea festival 113, 191
Seattle Design Nerds 18, *18*
Second Dome 218, *218, 219*
SelgasCano 131, *131*
Serpentine Pavilion 179, *179*
Seung Jin Yang 266, *266, 267*
Shaw, Jeffrey 182
Shenzhen Hong Kong Biennale (2009) 108, *108–9*
Shinseon Play 32, *32, 33*
SiloSilo 160, *160*
Skum 46, *46–7*
Sky Art Event 247, *247*
Sky Whale 193, *193*
Sleeping Bag Dress 194, *194, 195*
Slow Studio 25, *25*
Smigla-Bobinski, Karina 85, *85*
Snarkitecture 154, *154*
Snøhetta
    Stillspotting Guggenheim 233, *233*
    Tuballoon 206, *206*
Snoozy 189, *189*
Snowballing Doorway 21, *21*
Sodeau, Mike 128, 237, *237*
SolarPuff 251, *251*
The Soltz 217
Soufflet 190, *190*
Sound of Light 132, *132, 133*
space 12
Spacebuster 112, *112*
Spatial Effects 182
    Waterwalks 9, 162, *162, 163*
Speech Bubble 89
The Standard Hotel 79
Stanford University 56
Star Vase 128, *129*
Starck, Phillipe 185, *185*
State Garden Show, Wolfsburg 70
Stevens, Albert 8
Stillspotting Guggenheim 233, *233*
Storefront for Art and Architecture 112
stratospheric balloons 12
String Vienna 184, *184*

Studio GGSV 245, *245*
Studio MMASA 188, *188*
Stuffed Full 152, *152*
Suited for Subversion 136, *136*
Summer Igloo 68, *68*
superKOLMEMEN 53, *53*

T

Tafla Mirrors 44, *44*
Take My Hand, Rights and Weddings 114, *114*
Takizawa, Naoki 178, *178*
tanks, decoy 8, 208
Tastet, Benoît 155, *155*
Tate Modern, London 110
Tatton Park Biennial 221
teamLab
    Homogenizing and Transforming World 10, 94, *94, 95*
Tee Haus 141, *141*
Tel Aviv Museum of Art, Israel 264
telecommunications 12
Temporary Playground 70, *70*
Tenara 141
thermoplastic polyurethane (TPU) 157
Thirst Pavilion 36, *36*
Tight Spot 168, *168*
Timeline 255, *255*
Toer 151, *151*
Topotek 1 70, *70*
Towered 262, *262*
Traft 157, *157*
Transformable Armchair Jacket 192, *192*
Travelling Museum 31, *31*
Triennale Design Museum, Milan 172
Tuballoon 206, *206*
Typhon 229

U

UNESCO World Heritage Site 197

Uniblow Outfits 244, *244*
University of Arizona 13
Untitled (Hans Hemmert) 176, *176*
Untitled (Plastique Fantastique) 260, *260*
Urban Lights Ruhr festival 132

V

Vancil, Darren 156, *156*
Venice Biennale 75, 238
Verpan 90
Via Lattea 54, *54–5*
Victoria and Albert Museum, London 130
Video Folly 150, *150*
Villa Rosa 9
Villa Walala Exchange Square 76, *76*
Virilio, Paul 41
Vitra Design Museum 130
Vives, Carolina González 177, *177*
Vogler, Andreas 42, *42*
Volatile Structures 84, *84*
Voltaire 7
Vora Arquitectura 258, *258*

W

Walala, Camille 76, *76*
Walking in the Balloon 256, *256, 257*
Wall to Wall, Floor to Ceiling 264, *264*
Wanders, Marcel 11, 65, *65*
warfare 8–9
Warhol, Andy 238
Water Cube 26, *26–7*
Waterwalks 162, *162, 163*
weather balloons 12
The Wedge 43, *43*
White Drama 228, *228*
Wine Rack 128, *128*
With the Wind 108, *108–9*
Womanly 22, *22*
Wonderland 97, *97*
Worcester Art Museum, Massachusetts 243

World War I 8
World War II 8, 208
Wright, Frank Lloyd 9

Y

Yael Reisner Studio 114, *114*
Yamamoto, Yohji 64, *64*
You Wear What I Wear
 171, *171*
Young Architects Program
 (YAP) 32

Z

Zamarbide, Daniel 41, *41*
Zamproni, Geraldo
 Cosy Structure 191, *191*
 Volatile Structures
 84, *84*
Zanotta
 Blow Chair 11, 77, 130, *130*
Zeppelin, Count Ferdinand
 von 7–8
zeppelins 7–8
Zero2infinity 12
Zieta Prozessdesign Studio 11
 NAWA 270, *270–1*
 Plopp Stool 224, *224*, *225*
 Tafla Mirrors 44, *44*

Author Acknowledgements

Thanks to Phoebe for so much love and so
many life lessons; to Wally, I couldn't have done
this without you; to Nully and Colly, I couldn't
have done anything without you both; to Affy
and Daz for holding down the fort while I'm
AWOL; to V and C and D for being there for me;
and to Virginia and Belle at Phaidon for making
it happen. Love and gratitude.

Picture Credits

Kiri-Una Brito Meumann 22
Kristopher McKay, Courtesy of Solomon R. Guggenheim Museum, New York 233
Kristy Sparow/Getty Images 96
Kurt Perschke 101
Kyungsub Shin 32, 33
L/B 197, 242, 246
Lambert Kamps 73, 147, 150, 198, 269
Laurent Wangermez 181
Loop.pH 202, 203
Luca Fregoso 192
© Luis Ros 93
Malafor 92
Marcel Wanders 65
Marcella Grassi 114
Marco Barotti 111
Marjolein Fase 158
Markus Haugg 154
Markus Marty 79
Marty Melville/AFP/Getty Images 169
Mary Hale 170
Melissa Berry 200
© Meritalia 54-55
Michael Rakowitz 222
Michel Euler/AP 178
Moris Moreno 250
MOS Architects 238-239
Mossine Partners 159
Museum für Gestaltung, Zürich 224
Nacho Uribe Salazar 177
Namuun Zimmerman 99
© Nathan Willock/VIEW 261
Neilson Barnard/Getty Images for Chromat 72
Numen/Foruse 50
Numen/Foruse 184
O.T., 1998, (Latexballoon/Air/Museum, 900 x 550 x 650 cm, Installation view, CGAC Santiago de Compostella, Spain. © DACS 2018 176
© Offecct 57
Olivier Grossetete 221
Overtreders W 201
Paul Kozlowski 232

© Paul Litherland 20
Penttinen Schöne 140
Peter Fedrizzi 265
Photo by Douglas Adesko 248
Photo: Jimmy Söderling, © GORA art&landscape 259
© photoarchitecture.com 155
© Pierre Antoine 228
Pierre Leguillon 42
Pieter Boersma 163 top
Prisma by Dukas Presseagentur GmbH/Alamy Stock Photo 36
Rasmus Hjortshoj 46-47
Riccardo Bianchini/Alamy Stock Photo 75
© Richard-Max Trembla 195
Robert Sannes 206
Robyn Smith 113
Sean Gilligan 214
Sergio Grazia 30
Seungjin Yang 266, 267
Shih Chieh Huang 243
Solight Design 251
Stefan Leitner 43
Stefan Zeisler 249
Stephan Gottlicher 62
Steve Messam 24, 262
© Steve Topping 207
Studio Bertjan Pot 118
© StudioGGSV 245
Sully Balmassière, Courtesy of Copperfield, London 263
teamLab, courtesy of Pace gallery 94-95
The Asahi Shimbun via Getty Images 88
Theo Botschuijver 162
Theo Möller 86
Thomas Herzig 211
Toer 151
TOLGA AKMEN/AFP/Getty Images 34
Tom Vack 87
Tone Georgsen 241
Traft 157
Trevor Dykstra 18
University of California, Berkeley Art Museum and Pacific Film Archive. Photo: Chip Lord 223

Velvet Galerie 172, 173
Velvet Galerie 226
Victorine Müller 83
Vincent Gu 25
Virginia Melnyk 68
Wolfgang Volz 134

Phaidon Press Limited
Regent's Wharf
All Saints Street
London N1 9PA

Phaidon Press Inc.
65 Bleecker Street
New York, NY 10012

phaidon.com

First published 2019
© 2019 Phaidon Press Limited

ISBN 978 0 7148 7777 8

A CIP catalogue record for this book is available
from the British Library and the Library of Congress.

Commissioning Editor: Virginia McLeod
Project Editor: Belle Place
Production Controller: Sarah Kramer
Picture Researcher: Annalaura Palma

Design: StudioKanna

The Publisher would also like to thank Flavia Barbera,
Vanessa Bird, Ella Boardman, Eve Marleau, Michela
Parkin and Rebecca Roke for their contributions
to the book.

Front cover: *Homogenising and Transforming World*
by teamLab, 2014. Photo: Courtesy of Pace Gallery
Back cover: Air Flower by Fabrice Berrux for Roche
Bobois, 2013. Photo: Courtesy of Roche Bobois

Printed in China